ACCOUNTABILITY OR FREEDOM FOR TEACHERS?

ACCOUNTABILITY OR FREEDOM FOR TEACHERS?

Donald Bligh
(Editor)

Norman Lindop   Neil Merritt   Brian Gowenlock
and David Warren Piper
Mary Warnock

SOCIETY FOR RESEARCH INTO HIGHER EDUCATION

Research into Higher Education Monographs

The Society for Research into Higher Education,
At the University, Guildford, Surrey GU2 5XH

First published 1982

© 1982 The Society for Research into Higher Education

ISBN 0 900868 88 0

Printed in England by Direct Design (Bournemouth) Ltd. Printers
Butts Pond Industrial Estate, Sturminster Newton,
Dorset DT10 1AZ

THE LEVERHULME PROGRAMME
OF
STUDY INTO THE FUTURE OF HIGHER EDUCATION

This is the seventh publication of a programme of study focusing informed opinion and recent research findings on the major strategic options likely to be available to higher education institutions and policy-making bodies in the 1980s and 1990s. The programme as a whole has been made possible by a generous grant from the Leverhulme Trust to the Society for Research into Higher Education and is entirely independent of governmental or other organizational pressure. The present monograph is the second of two arising out of a specialist seminar on the teaching function in higher education. We are extremely grateful to Sir Bruce Williams, Director of the Technical Change Centre, for his excellent chairmanship as well as for his considerable interest in the whole programme.

A fundamental question facing higher education is the extent to which consensual arrangements and assumptions that generally worked well during the longer postwar period of its expansion can cope with the much more stringent conditions likely to prevail in the 1980s and 1990s. Is there sufficient common purpose amongst the various institutions and interest groups that constitute 'the higher education system' to permit the development of viable long-run policy objectives, or must higher education policy increasingly become merely the outcome of a struggle for survival and dominance among conflicting interests and ideas?

This is both a substantive and a methodological question. Substantively it will be faced squarely in the final report of the programme of study. Methodologically it will be tackled in the way the conclusions of that final report are reached.

In brief, the study is an experiment in formulating long-term strategies openly, taking into account the best available specialist knowledge about a complex system, the legitimate interests of a wide range of conflicting pressure groups, and wider public interests as perceived by disinterested individuals with no direct day-to-day involvement in higher education. The final recommendations will be the result of an iterative process in which proposals are made, then discussed, then revised, then reconsidered. Stage One is to commission research reviews by acknowledged experts in various specialist areas. Stage Two is a seminar at which others with detailed knowledge and experience of the area discuss these reviews. Stage Three is publication of the reviews together with a report of the discussion and of the policy implications highlighted by it. Stage Four is wider debate in the press and in specially convened conferences. Stage Five is reconsideration of the policy issues in the light of the wider reaction. Stage Six is the preparation of a final report. A seventh stage is of course hoped for, in which public authorities and institutions of higher education will take up the report's recommendations.

Publication of this monograph, together with its predecessor, the sixth in the SRHE Leverhulme series, represents the conclusion of the first three stages in that part of the programme concerned with the teaching function in higher education.

Other volumes in the series dealt with higher education and the labour market, access to higher education, institutional change in higher education, the future of research, the arts and higher education and professionalism and flexibility for learning.

The reports on all the seminars, together with comments on them from interested organizations and individuals, will form the basis for a final report setting out the conclusions and policy recommendations of the programme as a whole. This will be drawn up by the chairmen of the seminars and the editors of the accompanying monographs under the chairmanship of Lord Scarman and will be published in June 1983.

The scope of the Leverhulme programme is very wide. The need for a major review of higher education has been recognized by informed commentators for some time, and the financial stringency of recent years has made this need even more apparent. In its report *The Funding and Organization of Courses in Higher Education* the Education, Science and Arts Committee of the House of Commons commended the SRHE Leverhulme programme of study and concluded, 'We believe that higher education is at a watershed in its development and that the time is ripe for a great national debate....' The SRHE Leverhulme programme is intended to contribute to that debate by offering both a structure within which the main issues can be considered and an assessment of the evidence on which future policy should be based.

Gareth Williams
Programme Director

FOREWORD

by Sir Bruce Williams

The SRHE Leverhulme seminar on the teaching function in higher education institutions — the sixth in the series — discussed problems of teaching, learning and examining. In recent years there has been considerable criticism of staff performance in teaching and examining and of student performance in learning. There has also been a keener research interest in the three activities and, indeed, some of the criticism has arisen from that research.

Teaching performance has been criticized on the grounds that teachers (or some, or many, of them) are unclear or misguided about objectives, and do not give sufficient thought to the learning processes of students. In the case of universities a futher complaint is often heard — namely that the postwar growth of emphasis on research has led to a contraction of interest in teaching undergraduates.

Although criticism of examining is not new, the extent of criticism has increased. There are criticisms that students vary in their response to different forms of exams, that different examiners often give very different marks, that many examiners cannot give a clear account of what they are trying to test, and that what should be tested cannot be summed up adequately in one number or letter. As judged by the extent of change in methods of examining in the past fifteen years, these criticisms have been taken more seriously by staff. But this response to criticism has induced a further criticism that not enough has been done to test the efficacy of the new methods.

Criticism of the performance of the students' learning may be directed at the students for lack of motivation or knowhow, or at the staff for failing to motivate them (or to give appropriate tests of entry) or to provide adequate opportunities to acquire the knowhow. These are fields in which criticism is easy to make and in one sense to justify. But despite a considerable amount of research into the learning process our understanding of it is far from complete, and that is an indication of the difficulties involved in improving performance.

However, it is reasonable to assume that the process of teaching, learning and examining can be improved, and the seminar papers published in the sixth and seventh volumes in the SRHE Leverhulme series contain some important proposals for reform.

Most academics have highly developed critical capacities, though the balance between their critical activities directed inwards and outwards is not always optimal. But when they do get down to critizing teaching and examining activities they can be very fierce — at the seminar there were several occasions when I thought it right to protest that there is some very good teaching and examining, that there are some very good examples of well considered new approaches to teaching and examining in which care has been taken to provide for a running appraisal, and there is some very effective learning.

It would be wrong to give the impression that there are generally grave deficiencies in teaching, examining and learning. Doubtless there is room for improvement, and I hope that these SRHE Leverhulme volumes will stimulate improvements.

Bruce Williams
Chairman

CONTENTS

INTRODUCTION AND ACKNOWLEDGEMENTS 7

SEMINAR PARTICIPANTS 9

1 TEACHERS AND STAFFING 11
by Norman Lindop, Neil Merritt, Brian Gowenlock
and David Warren Piper

Introduction — The individual staff member — The
institutional setting — The national context — Summary
and proposals

2 THE PROFESSIONAL DEVELOPMENT OF TEACHING? 55
by Donald Bligh

The professional development of teaching needs to be
planned — Plans to change and improve teaching will
need to be based on methods shown to be feasible —
Plans must obtain the commitment of social and working
groups — The difficulties in implementing professional
development plans need to be recognized at a senior level —
There is a need to institutionalize professional
development — The changes needed require a central
initiative — Conclusions

3 THE VALUES PRESUPPOSED 100
by Mary Warnock

The future of the binary system — The curriculum —
Academic freedom

4 FREEDOMS, RIGHTS AND ACCOUNTABILITY 118
by Donald Bligh

What academic freedoms in teaching can be justified? —
A contract between student and institution? — How and
to whom are teachers accountable? — Conclusion

INTRODUCTION AND ACKNOWLEDGEMENTS

Educational policies are not formed in vacuo. They emerge from a climate of opinion created in discussion and publication. The SRHE Leverhulme series of seminars and monographs is a major new contribution to that climate of opinion.

This is the second of the two SRHE Leverhulme monographs containing papers submitted to the seminar on the teaching function of higher education. It is more concerned with teachers than with students.

It raises issues that need to be resolved by consensus. Its propositions are starters for discussion for any group of academic staff, provided the group can go beyond them to form policy recommendations of its own.

Chapter 1 begins with a review of the varied contexts and conditions of the work of academic staff. It uncovers a variety of problems and then considers a number of propositions for solving them; but it does not make recommendations. The word 'proposition' is intended as a neutral term. The propositions can be discussed separately or several at a time.

Chapter 2 adopts a more traditional approach to decisions. First the needs of professional development are described. Present approaches and policies to satisfy them are summarized. Two sections outline the necessary conditions and contexts for a policy. The last two sections consider general proposals in the context of higher education institutions and of the higher education system as a whole. Some of these proposals have since been echoed in a pamphlet produced by the Association of University Teachers in 1982 called *The Professional Development and Training of University Teachers*.

Mary Warnock's brief in Chapter 3 was to comment on the values presupposed in this and the first of the two volumes on the teaching function. She selected three issues for consideration: the structure of higher education; the content and methods of the curriculum; and conflicting demands for the academic freedom and social accountability of teachers.

The last of these issues, freedom or accountability, underlies many that are raised in the first two chapters of this book. It is therefore taken up for closer examination in the final chapter and gives its name to the volume as a whole.

ACKNOWLEDGEMENTS

The consultative process in the preparation of this and the previous monograph in the SRHE Leverhulme series means that there are many people to be thanked for their contributions.

I am most grateful to Professor Gareth Williams for his support and advice on the procedure I have adopted, to Sir Bruce Williams for his quiet, authoritative chairmanship, to all the authors whose ideas and written contributions were subjected to comment and criticism that was more than usually public in the early stages, to Miss Betty Hollinshead, Mr Trevor Habeshaw, Dr Alex Main, Professor Peter Ayscough and Dr David Armstrong for organizing fruitful pre-seminars so willingly and efficiently and without any thought of reward, to Mrs Betsy Breuer for her accommodating organization, to Sally Kington for her professional approach to the publication, to the University of Exeter for allowing me to spend so much time on this work, and most of all, to Mrs Lynne Griffiths who conquered the worst frustrations of mastering a word-processor and who has typed and re-typed not only many drafts of the chapters but many versions of the preliminary sheets, containing propositions, counter-propositions and their respective arguments, which contributed to the discussions from which the chapters eventually evolved.

Donald Bligh
Editor

SEMINAR PARTICIPANTS

   Sir Bruce Williams (Chairman)
* Dr David Armstrong, University of London
* Professor Peter Ayscough, University of Leeds
   Mr Ron Barnett, Council for National Academic Awards
   Professor Tony Becher, University of Sussex
   Professor Paul Black, Chelsea College, University of London
+ Dr Donald Bligh, University of Exeter (Convenor)
   Mr John Davidson, Bristol Polytechnic
   Professor Lewis Elton, University of Surrey
   Mr Norman Evans, Policy Studies Institute
   Mr Colin Flood Page
   Mr Dennis Fox, Trent Polytechnic
   Dr Sinclair Goodlad, Imperial College, University of London
   Dr Richard Hoggart, Goldsmiths' College, University of London
+ Sir Norman Lindop, Hatfield Polytechnic
*Dr Alex Main, University of Strathclyde
   Dr Alan Matterson, Kingston Polytechnic
   Professor Emeritus Roy Niblett
   Mr John O'Leary, *The Times Higher Education Supplement*
   Mr Andrew Pearmain, National Union of Students
   Mrs Pauline Perry, Department of Education and Science
   Professor Sir Brian Pippard, University of Cambridge
   Dr Anthony Pointon, Association of Polytechnic Teachers
   Professor Alec Ross, University of Lancaster
   Ms. Patricia Santinelli, *The Times Higher Education Supplement*
   Mr Richard Smethurst, University of Oxford
   Professor John Sparkes, The Open University
   Dr Geoffrey Squires, University of Hull
   Professor Michael Stephens, University of Nottingham
   Professor Campbell Stewart, University of Sussex
   Dr Graham Stodd, West Sussex Institute of Higher Education
   Mr John Taylor, Advisory Council for Adult and Continuing Education
   Dr William Taylor, University of London Institute of Education
   Mr Malcolm Tight, Birkbeck College, University of London
+ Mrs Mary Warnock, Hertford College, University of Oxford
+ Mr David Warren Piper, University of London Institute of Education
   Professor Gareth Williams, University of Lancaster

+ Author of paper   * Convenor of pre-seminar

1

TEACHERS AND STAFFING

by Norman Lindop, Neil Merritt, Brian Gowenlock and David Warren Piper

IMPORTANT NOTE
This chapter has no single author; it is the result of consultations and individual drafting by Norman Lindop, Brian Gowenlock, Neil Merritt, and David Warren Piper and some editorial work by Norman Lindop, Donald Bligh and David Warren Piper. The intention was to propose issues for further discussion, *not* to make formal proposals. It should not be assumed that each of the proposals mentioned is supported by all four contributors.

The following acronyms are used:

ABRC	Advisory Board for the Research Councils
AFE	Advanced Further Education
BEC	Business Education Council
CNAA	Council for National Academic Awards
DES	Department of Education and Science
SRHE	Society for Research into Higher Education
TEC	Technician Education Council
UGC	University Grants Committee

INTRODUCTION
The higher education system exists because of the work of the academic staff, and it has grown by their efforts. It is based upon their expertise and upon their concept of what constitutes higher education. Over the past half-century, new developments have constantly emerged as a result of their activities. Decisions by administrators or politicians may have facilitated and encouraged these developments, but it has been the academics who have determined the essential characteristics of the system. Until a few years ago the public climate in which academics in higher education worked was almost wholly favourable. Not only were those within the universities granted academic autonomy and self-determination almost without question, but these traditions were fostered and encouraged in the newly developed public sector institutions, and the resources to finance an expansion in line with the comparatively generous Robbins Principle were made available. There was a consensus support for the system. From 1975 onwards the autonomy, traditions and consensus have been breaking down under the strains put upon resources and in a crisis of self-doubt.

The very people who by their skills and professionalisms have built up the higher education system now find themselves exposed. The costs and benefits of the whole higher education sector are being called into question. The academic staff themselves are the most vulnerable and expensive components. Far from being able to retreat into ivory towers and ignore public comment, they now find themselves in a hostile political climate, having to defend themselves as well as the system they helped to create. As teachers they are finding themselves exposed to public questioning and criticism. They find that their assertions of professional competence to carry out the responsibilities of their autonomy are not automatically accepted. External criteria and sanctions are expected. This new social context, uncomfortable though it is, has come to stay. Even the hallowed assumption that everyone in the profession is at least minimally competent is called in question. Public accountability must now be satisfied in addition to the traditional accountability of the academic to scholarship.

The profession of teachers and researchers in higher education is deeply divided by history, by tradition, and by administrative and political arrangements. The universities are basically financed nationally, through a single central body for the whole of the UK. Consequently, university staff form a reasonably homogeneous major group, although each individual owes allegiance to a particular institution as employer, a particular departmental group and a particular subject-area. The rest of the so-called binary system is divided into a small number of centrally or privately funded institutions, and a large number of local authority institutions, including the polytechnics, which are, at least nominally, locally financed. Here again the individual finds his loyalty closest to his daily work. The objectives of the different types of higher education institutions across the binary system are said to be distinct and separately defensible (though in practice blurring seems to occur) and the administrative and financial traditions are totally different. The effect is that what might have become a single unified profession is deeply split in a number of different ways. Inevitably this makes the discussion of academic staff problems fragmented.

In this chapter we consider first the individual staff member, secondly the institutional setting in which he works, and finally the higher education system. Into this discursive text we have inserted a few facts and figures about staff in this country. We end with a section which is partly a summary but mostly a list of propositions which we hope will provoke discussion. We have chosen the word 'proposition' carefully, not wishing to imply that they are recommendations which would be wholly endorsed either by members of the seminar or by the Society for Research into Higher Education (SRHE). We are conscious that in considering the institutional and national context of the teacher's working life we are necessarily intruding on some of the matters considered in the third book arising from the SRHE Leverhulme programme, that is *Agenda for Institutional Change in Higher Education* edited by Leslie Wagner.

THE INDIVIDUAL STAFF MEMBER

The Job of the Academic
The idea of a university is based upon a community of scholars. The job of the university teacher is commonly described in terms of two major commitments, teaching and research, which are usually said to be of comparable importance. These two activities overlap and fuse in the postgraduate area. The pursuit of high quality research is an axiomatic activity for universities, and the personal element of research is important for the individual teacher's intellectual and career development. In the competition for senior posts an academic's personal research record is at least as important as teaching performance — most people believe it is more so. The result is a curious and possibly unique relationship between the individual and the organization within which he is employed. A university teacher's standing among the academic community, and thus his perceived value to his university, does not depend upon how well he or she contributes to the corporate activity of the university, its teaching, even though a great portion of the public monies contributed to the higher education system is earmarked for this purpose.

One of the major functions of universities is to provide a base for the activities of scholars of national and international stature and repute. Universities must be seen to facilitate scholarly work of originality and significance and to be educating the scholars of the future. Ninety-three per cent of university staff appear to be involved in scholarly or research work at any one time. At the same time much of the teaching of undergraduate students has to be done at a more mundane level. The varied levels of students' work can create difficulties for teachers. For example the teaching of ancillary or subsidiary subjects, which may be essential components of courses, can seem unexciting to specialists and may add little or nothing to their career prospects. Despite the fact that 52 per cent of university staff (compared with only 19 per cent of polytechnic staff) report their prime interest to lie in research, only 28 per cent agree that their first loyalty should be to research rather than to teaching and administration (the comparable figure for polytechnics is 10 per cent) (Halsey 1980).

There is a constant tension for the individual, for departments and for whole institutions, between the twin commitments to teaching and research. Because the teaching of the students has to be formally timetabled, personal research has to be fitted round it; and research can suffer when there is a heavy teaching commitment. Forty-six per cent of university staff and 65 per cent of polytechnic staff report a degree of uneasiness about the amount of time they are able to devote to research because of the teaching demands made upon them (Halsey 1980). In some disciplines consultancy ensures that staff keep professionally up-to-date, keeps them in touch with developments outside their academic domain, maintains their professional credibility, enriches their teaching and research with socially relevant problems, and provides them with additional income.

Within the teaching function itself universities are by tradition (and by virtue of their charters) autonomous and self-validating, so that course objectives, curricula, and standards of awards are all determined by the teaching staff. The main mechanisms for peer evaluation and judgement are the internal processes of academic democracy and the system of external examiners. Both, at their best, can be very effective, constituting a rigorous framework within which the work of the individual teacher is sensitively monitored and controlled. The mechanisms can also, on occasion, be less reliable, permitting idiosyncratic variations and a lack of rigour. Nevertheless, there has been acceptance nationally that all university degrees indicate a broadly equivalent standard of professional or educational competence; or at least that none fall below a satisfactory standard. This widespread acceptance of internally determined standards is a distinguishing feature of the British university system. Within the universities it is a matter of justifiable pride and satisfaction that it is so, and the academic staff of the universities rightly set great store by it. It must be a question for debate whether so diffuse a set of mechanisms can keep the system on course as resource constraints become tighter. Nevertheless, the seminar recommended an extension of peer review mechanisms.

Most polytechnic teachers would claim that the particular nature of their job is based upon students' demands for diverse courses and patterns of study at a variety of levels, and students' expectations that courses will be relevant to their employment and their careers. A high proportion of polytechnic staff has at some time practised a profession outside academe, though for some it may be a rather distant memory. Their job is primarily seen to be that of teaching, and the broader range of levels of work is accepted as part of the commitment. Research is done in most departments, though not necessarily by all staff. Although it is often stated that staff are expected to do research there is less material encouragement for it than in universities; for example there has never been any attempt to introduce a counterpart of the universities' (now threatened) 'dual support' system. Nevertheless, 60 per cent of staff claim to be currently engaged in work expected to lead to publication. Even so, the complaint is sometimes made that research is a more weighty factor in promotion than the declared aims of the institutions would justify. The teaching carried out by a typical polytechnic teacher is probably more diverse than that of his university counterpart. This is partly because the work of the institution is itself more diverse, with considerable effort spent on part-time courses, sandwich course placements and supervision, and short courses. The tradition of long teaching hours and, in some instances, the (perhaps excessive) proliferation of administration and committee work contributes to the diversity and adds to the load.

One of the most strongly marked differences between university and non-university institutions is in the teaching load (as measured in contact hours per week, say) of staff. The average load for university staff is lower than that for staff in the other sector. University staff on average spend 37 per cent of their time on undergraduate and postgraduate teaching, whereas polytechnic staff spend 53 per cent teaching at various levels (Halsey 1980). The reasons for this are no doubt complex and they must include the commitment of universities and their staff to research, traditions in further education whereby staff effort is measured entirely by contact hours, the consequent tendency to over-teach, and differences in the quality and expectations of students.

One of the strongest influences on the teaching staff in all types of public sector higher education institutions during the past two decades has been that of the validating bodies, especially CNAA, TEC, BEC, and, in one or two cases, universities. The main effects of CNAA validation have been to put squarely upon the teachers the responsibility for the design of courses and their defence before peer evaluators; to give teachers responsibility for the operation and monitoring of courses, and for the admission, teaching and assessment of students; and to use external examiners in much the same way as in the universities.

The new validation climate has offered new opportunities as well as new responsibilities. Much curriculum innovation has been carried out — so much, in fact, that curriculum development, validation and monitoring have become major preoccupations of staff, sometimes even to the detriment of their teaching. There is something of a validation industry. At the same time it has to be acknowledged that in facilitating and encouraging the development of genuine peer evaluation in the public sector institutions (where it formerly hardly existed) this validation industry has had beneficial effects. Both academic staff and the institutions themselves have matured far more rapidly than traditional modes of tutelage would have allowed. The benefits of peer evaluation of teaching should not be ignored by other sections of higher education.

Staff Structure
The higher education teaching profession was a comparatively small one before the Second World War. Although its numbers had doubled between 1910 and 1930, and doubled again by 1949, there were still only about 8,000 university teachers by that date. Thereafter expansion quickened and the total grew rapidly. It had doubled again by 1963 and again by 1975, by which time the brakes were being applied. Thereafter numbers levelled out (see Figure 1.1).

In the non-university sector the upheavals, mergers and closures of the last fifteen years make comparisons of staff numbers extremely difficult to calculate and in many cases of doubtful value — many institutions have suffered fundamental changes, and the line which runs through most of them, dividing 'advanced' from 'non-advanced' further education, has

TABLE 1.1
Age distribution of teaching staff

Age		Universities %			Polytechnics %
		1961/2	1968	1980	1980
−25		5.3	2.6	2.8	0.25
26−30		17.2	17.7	8.8	4.9
31−35		20.6	21.0	19.6	17.6
36−40		20.7	16.4	20.0	17.5
41−45		12.4	14.7	13.0	18.4
46−50		9.5	11.2	12.5	17.1
51−55		6.6	6.7	10.3	13.0
56−60		4.7		7.2	8.1
61−65		2.6	9.7	5.5	3.1
66+		0.4		0.3	0.15
30 or under	%	22.5	20.3	11.6	5.15
	No.	3,290	5,400	3,840	880
40 or under	%	63.8	57.7	51.2	40.25
	No.	9,360	15,350	16,900	6,900
Over 50	%	14.3	16.4	23.3	24.35
	No.	14,640	26,650	33,000	4,170

moved correspondingly, so that comparable figures for staff engaged on higher education cannot be extracted. Only for the polytechnics (and even then only recently) are figures of any value available.

A profession which experiences very different rates of growth at different times inevitably shows an age profile which is markedly different from a profession which has enjoyed a 'steady state' or an equilibrium between recruitment and wastage over a number of years. The exceptional surge of growth in the mid- and late 1960s, which has been followed by a relative stasis or even a decline in numbers has resulted in an age profile which presents severe problems to individuals and to institutions, especially at a time when retrenchment is required. The profile varies from subject to subject, depending upon whether, and at what date, student demand faltered. The natural and applied sciences had an uneasy time in the early 1970s, when social sciences were still forging ahead.

TABLE 1.2
University and public sector pay from 1st April 1981

UNIVERSITY	£	PUBLIC SECTOR	£
Lecturer	6,066 – 12,860	LII/SL	6,463 – 12,140
SL/Reader	12,305 – 15,408	PL/Reader	11,297 – 14,238
Professor (average)	18,477	HOD VI	15,045 – 16,490

TABLE 1.3
The distribution of academic staff amongst grades in universities and polytechnics

	Universities %	Polytechnics %	Other maintained establishments No.	%
Directors/ principals	-	0.18	558	
Deputies, assistant directors & vice-principals	-	0.73	507	6.0
Heads of department	-	4.35	2544	
University professors	12.5	-	-	
University readers/ senior lecturers	23.7	-	-	
Non-university readers/ principal lecturers	-	19.2	3236	5.4
Total senior staff	36.2	24.5		11.4
University lecturers/ assistant lecturers	61.1	-	-	
Senior lecturers/ lecturer II	-	72.0	13995	23.4
Others: lecturer I demonstrators, research assistants, etc.	2.7	3.5	22336	37.4

If it is assumed that staff numbers are currently stable because of the financial conditions now imposed, it will become necessary for an institution to plan its staffing procedures and the age distribution of its staff in a rational pattern. It seems very difficult for this activity to be compatible with life-time tenure. A department may have staff who are very suitable for the jobs they are now doing, but entirely within the 40—55 age range. In a time of no growth such a department might appoint no new staff for ten years. The problems of departments of this type are apparent, and there is little expertise in dealing with them at the present time. If they are to be avoided, policies will be necessary to make new appointments possible and to develop the transfer of staff between institutions, which seems preferable to setting up large schemes. The scope for research council funding of such activities may well be small and only affect a minority of departments and disciplines. Nevertheless, the national situation must be tackled. The overall age distribution of academic staffs shown in Figure 1.2 is such that there are too many staff in the 35—45 age group. If policies for meeting present financial difficulties do not lead to a marked diminution of this group, then flexibility in dealing with the problems of the 1990s will disappear, because of considerable use of early retirement amongst the present 55+ age group. Those institutions which tackle the problem of age distribution will have an enhanced flexibility to deal with staffing problems in ten years time and will also be able to recruit some members of the forthcoming generation of scholars throughout this decade.

In retrospect the problems of the age structure of the profession might have been avoided if, during the hectic expansion, more varied ages had been recruited. This would have required positive discrimination in favour of older candidates, whereas the natural tendency is to appoint the young (cheap) and promising. Now there are complaints that the profession lacks the necessary proportion of 'young Turks', the clear-eyed thrusters of the new generation. Although there is something in this, the actual numbers of university academics under the age of thirty is still as high as twenty years ago (Table 1.1). What has certainly changed is the expectation that good young graduates/postgraduates will more or less automatically move on to teaching posts. In the late 1960s up to 60 per cent of each year's graduates was staying on to do postgraduate study (excluding teacher training) and over 70 per cent of first-class Honours scientists to do research — the progression from postgraduate to post-doctoral research was straightforward and the prospects of tenured academic posts was good. All is now changed; the number of vacancies has dwindled almost to zero and for the next few years, with redundancy stalking the campuses, the prospect of there being opportunities for the young entrants must depend on positive action to create openings in spite of the overall retrenchment.

One would not expect the age profiles for staff of public sector higher education institutions to correspond in detail with those of universities. It

TEACHERS AND STAFFING   19

FIGURE 1.1
Number of university teachers (GB) 1900 — 1980 (after Halsey and Trow 1971)

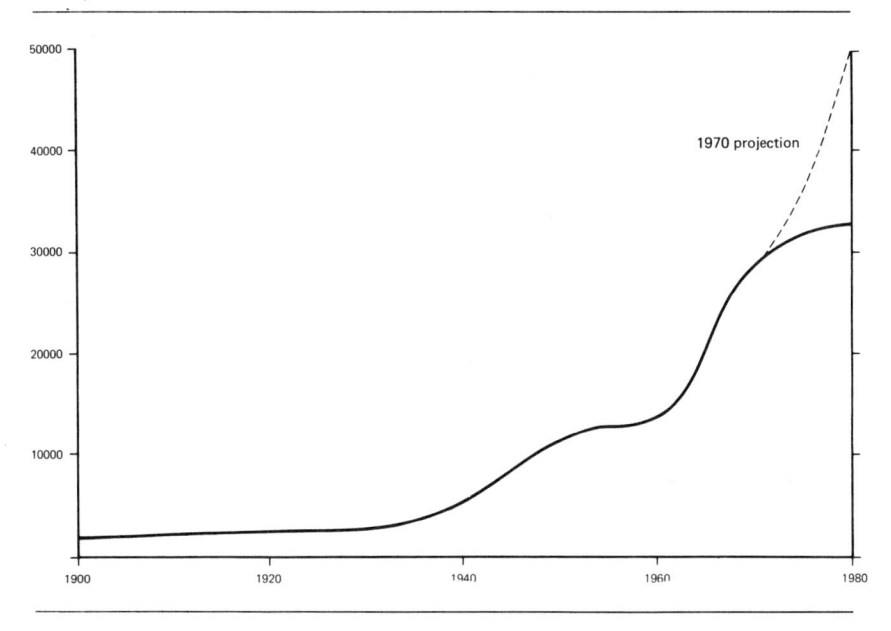

FIGURE 1.2
Age distribution of staff 1980

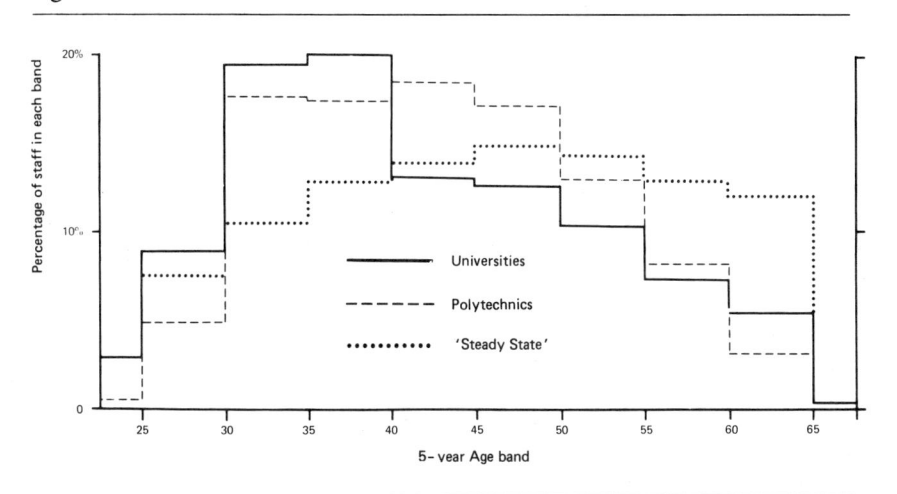

has always been the policy wherever possible in these institutions to recruit suitably qualified candidates who have also had some years of professional experience. Consequently, while this partly corresponds with the usual pattern of post-doctoral research preceding university appointments, the average age of first appointment has tended to be higher in public sector higher education establishments. This is borne out by the polytechnic figures in Table 1.1; the proportion of staff below 30 or below 40 is significantly lower in each case than in the universities while the proportion of staff in their 40s is markedly higher.

There is another consequence of the erratic growth of the profession on both sides of the binary line in the last twenty years: the quality of staff is likely to have been affected. It may be supposed that many staff recruited during the late 1960s (and, in the universities, recruited with expectation of tenure) were people of a calibre who would not have been appointed at earlier periods — and who would not be appointed now. Many of these people are now in their early 40s and could be in post for another twenty years. In all probability some subject areas are more affected by this phenomenon than others. It is possible, for example, that there were sufficient natural scientists of appropriate calibre to meet the recruitment demands of the late 60s without loss of quality, but it is also arguable that in other areas of rapid expansion, for example in the social sciences, the pool of ability was over-fished, especially by some institutions in the public sector. The consequences could be with us for a long time.

It is difficult to substantiate such trends statistically. Even supposing that the class of first degree and the possession of a PhD are valid indicators of academic quality, the figures need careful interpretation. For instance in universities between 1961 and 1971 the proportion of staff with first-class Honours degrees went down while the proportion with PhDs went up. Taken at their face value such figures are hard enough to interpret but various complications add to the difficulty. The category system used by the UGC to define academic staff changed between 1961 and 1969, admitting more research workers but, interestingly, fewer with first-class degrees. This decline in firsts may reflect the growth in the number of social science staff; a low proportion of these staff have first-class degrees, because few firsts were awarded by social science faculties. So even without over-fishing in social sciences, the pool of ability as defined by social science departments who award the degrees, is smaller than in, say, the physical sciences. High standards set by examiners lead directly to an apparent decline in academic standards of recruited staff (Williams, Blackstone and Metcalf 1974). Despite these complications, however, one might suppose that if there were a fall in standards it would show disproportionately in the public sector. Again the figures are equivocal. The universities now have 43 per cent of their staff with first-class Honours degrees because only 32 per cent of their new appointees between 1970 and 1976 had firsts. The polytechnics are left with 19 per cent with first-class Honours, having recruited 14 per cent with firsts over the same period. Certainly the universities have better qualified staff, but the rate of decline is only a little less than that of the polytechnics.

Whatever the statistical trends, over 60 per cent of university staff and over 70 per cent of polytechnic staff believe there is a pool of mediocre staff appointed in the 1960s now blocking the promotion of more able people (Halsey 1980).

In one respect the structure of the academic profession has changed little over the years — the percentage of women has remained remarkably low. For the universities it is around 11.5 while for the polytechnics it is 14.5; for further education generally it is 20.0 and in the former colleges of education in 1973 (before their absorption into the system) it was 31.6. There are marked variations in this proportion according to subject, women tending to be found mainly in the social sciences, humanities and education faculties — and also mainly in the lower paid posts.

The Employment Pattern

In virtually all institutions of higher education the academic structure and organization of the teaching staff follows the main subject divisions. In spite of a number of attempts to diffuse the boundaries inherent in a traditional departmental system, for example by using matrix structures, it is inevitable that the teachers think of themselves as practitioners of particular kinds and regard their academic home and base as a subject-group (see Chapter 2, pages 65 ff.). Teachers almost invariably have contracts of employment which relate to single specified institutions. Thus whatever commonality an analysis of jobs and functions may suggest that there is, the teaching profession in higher education is divided and subdivided to an extraordinary degree — by the binary line, by the nature of the employer or paymaster (UGC/LEA/DES/etc.), by institutional boundaries, by faculty, school and/or departmental boundaries, by broad subject allegiance, by specialist interest. Yet all, or nearly all, of these teachers believe (or until recently believed) themselves to be guaranteed a job for their normal working life — each entirely within his or her self-chosen subject-compartment, irrespective of the fortunes of the system or institution.

These were the assumptions of the relatively small, pre-Robbins, profession. They have been taken over by the enlarged profession of today, but the conditions for their realization (in particular, steady expansion) have disappeared. In the changed circumstances of today and tomorrow a question which must be asked is whether it will be necessary to consider a broader, less restricted basis of teacher employment in higher education — a unified profession, employed by 'the (national) higher education service', located in different institutions and organizational units, or perhaps each teacher jointly serving two or more. This would allow greater flexibility to adjust staffing to student numbers and subject demand within institutions and, once the system had achieved some sort of equilibrium, a more secure prospect of continuing employment for each teacher. There would clearly be losses — for example a blurring of institutional loyalties, the disorganization of personal lifestyles, and possibly the disturbance of teaching continuity; but there would be gains too — for example, the greater harmonization of practice and standards between institutions, the preservation of minority subject interests, and the sharing of the good specialist teachers. The sharing of specialist expertise between higher education institutions already occurs to a very limited extent. The proposal would regularize and systematize this sharing and make it more of a rule than an exception.

It is difficult to envisage such a major change in staffing procedures without a new approach to the overall organization, planning and control of the whole higher education system. If a new approach to the whole higher education system is not possible for other reasons, the proposed revision of employment arrangements is out of the question; but if a major change in this direction can be undertaken, this reform of staffing could follow naturally.

It would seem desirable that senior appointments (ie those at departmental and college/polytechnic/university principal level) should be made on a fixed contract basis with 'return-rights'. If such appointments were established the consequence could be that:

a More persons would be willing to undertake the leadership of departments and/or institutions.
b A greater understanding of the difficulties of leadership in departments and institutions could result.

The nature of the return-right is that the institution or system guarantees an appointee to a post of head of department or above the right to return to a teaching-level grade at a reduced salary (eg one-tenth less than the salary of the post held on a fixed time contract), together with tenure. National arrangements could be made whereby a person (say at the rank of principal or vice-chancellor) would, as of right, move to another institution as a teacher/researcher under the return-rights in the fixed term contract for the post. (To move to another institution would be a better arrangement because his successor would be unembarrassed by his presence.)

The introduction of such a system would bring at least two problems. First, persons whose contracts were not renewed would inevitably suffer loss of face. Loss of face could be avoided by establishing a principle that the period of the contract should be fixed and non-renewable. However such a principle would prevent able principals or vice-chancellors from continuing their service. Secondly, principals and vice-chancellors of undeniable but eccentric talents might be lost to the service as a consequence of capricious decisions by governing bodies.

Levels of Remuneration
When they came to discuss the level of remuneration and social status of university academics, Halsey and Trow (1971) suggested that the 'average' academic (a scientist aged 36 near the top of the lecturer grade) was comfortably within the top 10 per cent of earners — 'a secure member of the British middle classes'. Moreover, with relatively generous student/staff ratios and light formal obligations, he had an unusual degree of freedom in the sense of personal autonomy — a 'gentlemanly' way of life, in fact. He was motivated not only by his scholarly interests but by a desire for a good reputation as measured by peer evaluation and, sometimes, by the entrepreneurial desire to conduct a kind of private business within the framework of his university post. All this in a context of professionalism (based upon a secure income) so that he usually worked well beyond the unexacting minimum demands of his job, and regarded the maintenance of standards as a major responsibility.

A decade later much of this picture is intact, though the pressures have certainly increased. Whatever the anomalies and disappointments on questions to do with their salaries, teachers in higher education still have what most people would regard as an enviable life. Teachers in the public sector of higher education have also felt the pressures. They are linked to the main body of teachers in further education as far as salary scales are concerned, and they inherit rather different traditions and styles of work from university teachers. Increased teaching loads, as measured by student/staff ratios (which have virtually doubled during the last decade) have come to dominate the scene. Acrimony has occasionally broken out across the binary line when one group has 'leap-frogged' the other in the haphazard timing of salary settlements. The public sector, in particular, experienced something of a step-function at the time of the Houghton (1974) and Clegg (1980) awards. Nevertheless, the general picture has remained, in which, while salary scales at lower levels have a rough comparability across the line, there are considerable discrepancies at senior levels (Table 1.2). In public sector higher education there is no equivalent to the broad band of professorial salaries, and the proportion of senior staff is markedly lower than in the universities (Table 1.3). In effect, therefore, in spite of some apparent correspondence in scales, the average salaries in polytechnics and colleges are lower than those in universities.

While the proportion of senior posts amongst academic staff is roughly similar across the university system, there is no uniformity on the other side of the binary line. An appendix to the annual report of the Burnham Committee gives broad bands of percentages of senior staff in institutions carrying out advanced work, and there is wide variation in practice even between apparently similar institutions within the public sector. Across the binary line there are considerable differences in the distribution of staff over the seniority scales. Ten per cent of university staff are professors; four per cent of polytechnic staff are departmental heads. Readers and senior lecturers make up one-quarter of the univeristy staff, whereas the salary-equivalent grades of principal lecturer and reader account for just under one-fifth of polytechnic staff. About 60 per cent of university staff and 70 per cent of polytechnic staff are in the grades corresponding to university lecturer scales. In a survey of staff in a provincial university, Startup (1979) reported that 68 per cent of staff agreed 'wage for age' to be the best dominant principle for determining academic salaries. There was no wide support for any other principle despite the obvious lack of financial incentive in such schemes. Assuming similar atttudes elsewhere in the higher education system, a radical change in the salary structure would seem to be unpopular.

Conditions of Service
The conditions of service of staff have always differed across the binary line. The traditional conditions of university teachers were very loosely defined; the commitment of the individual to the values of scholarship was assumed to be a guarantee of satisfactory performance. The conditions of service for teachers in public sector higher education are partly derived from the patterns of service existing in schools, and modified, especially by the demands of part-time students for evening tuition. There has always been a tendency towards a rule-book approach, though this varies considerably from one institution to another according to the policy of the education authority, the principal and the attitude of the local branch of the teachers' union. Staff attitudes too, have varied greatly from one institution to another, in some cases being indistinguishable from those of university staff.

Whereas university teachers had (or in some cases until recently thought they had) something like 'life tenure', public sector higher education teachers have never had such a guarantee, and where redundancies have occurred the terms have varied considerably from case to case. Teachers in colleges of education, whose jobs disappeared because of government action in the 1970s, could, and in large numbers did, claim relatively generous compensation under the Crombie Code. In one or two instances, schemes for early retirement under voluntary redundancy procedures have been promoted by individual local education authorities in response to local financial emergencies, but there has been no national pattern, and such schemes have generally been less favourable to the individual than those now proposed for the university sector.

Apart from the redundancy situation, however, it is fair to say that employment legislation has conferred greater security of tenure on employees of all kinds than was formerly the case, and in this respect the two sectors are of course similar.

The increasing unionization of staff of all grades, which has accelerated during the financial blizzard, has introduced and emphasized new political constraints within institutions. Although the process is nowhere as advanced as is common in some European institutions, notably in Germany, in public sector higher education in this country there has been a politicization of some academic boards and governing bodies as well as of local education authorities, to the extent that the frontier of politics is now felt to run right through some of the public sector institutions, seriously affecting the academic process, limiting the discretion of academic staff even in the determination of curriculum details, and restricting the availability and functions of non-academic staff in support of the teaching function. These pressures have also been felt in the university system, though the institutions themselves have not lost their independence of the political world in the way that some public sector higher education institutions have, becoming political footballs at the mercy of local factions.

The role of staff in policy planning, and the role of trade union activities in respect of job security, can become blurred in the process of institutional democracy. This can weaken the credibility of an academic board as an organ of representation to the governing body and the maintaining authority. The absence of direct union negotiating arrangements with governing bodies of institutions in the public sector of higher education (except in ILEA polytechnics and polytechnics maintained by joint education committees) makes it more likely that the staff unions will use the academic board as part of the process of bringing pressure on authorities when loss of jobs is possible. Consideration should be given to the nature of union consultation with governing bodies in institutions of public sector higher education. There are at present great variations in practice. In some cases academic boards are much less effective as a result of their use by staff unions as vehicles for staff representation.

THE INSTITUTIONAL SETTING

Participative Management
In all higher education institutions academic staff are involved in activities variously described as administration, management, or participation in government or policy making. Implicit in the university's ideal of the self-governing collegium is the obligation to participate in policy making. At departmental level something in the region of two-thirds of both university and polytechnic staff regard their departmental administration as democratic (Halsey 1980). Yet the extent to which an individual undertakes these activities is often a matter of personal choice, though in the public sector at least the Burnham salary documents give support to the idea that administration is not only a recognized but a creditable activity, and this results in good teachers seeking promotion by doing less teaching and more administration (for which they are often untrained and occasionally unfitted). There are interesting differences here between the

universities and polytechnics. On the average, university staff claim to spend about a fifth of their time on administration, although a tenth would be their ideal. Polytechnic staff say that administration takes more than a quarter of their time, twice as much as their ideal (Halsey 1980). In an interesting study of one university, Startup (1979) reported that three-quarters of the staff said they liked doing administration at least a little, and that as many as 60 per cent felt that people in their grade ought to do more than they did. It seems people feel more guilty about not doing administration than not doing research. This makes sense if administration is a social commitment to those whom they meet daily, whereas research is an activitiy seeking prestige amongst a peer group which seldom meets as a body.

Most institutions depend upon a structure or network of committees, boards or working parties, partly to effect communication between different parts and levels of the organization, and partly to determine and implement policy by involving staff at all levels in consultative and judgemental processes. Such committees have been called the plumbing of the academic system — they are a necessary evil, which can however consume a disproportionate amount of the time of academic staff. If, however, management and policy decisions are not taken by academics, they are taken by full-time administrators and this produces tensions within institutions. In general, therefore, academics accept the necessity of joining in the processes of participative decision making.

Participative management has much to recommend it. People are likely to be more committed to policies which they have argued or at least heard argued in detail. Also the principle of participative management reflects the tradition of the universities as being a college of equals acting together in mutual interest. However, participative management works less well when staff are required to act, not on behalf of their colleagues, but on behalf of a key sector of the community by providing a major educational service.

Management by committee exhibits some peculiarities. In a committee no individual is responsible for the quality of the decisions made. Also it is common for a committee operating at a high level of management to be comprised of individuals who, if accountable at all, are accountable at a lower level of management, as when heads of departments form a committee (senate) to decide on the distribution of resources or the closure of a particular department. Indeed, the interests of the institution may conflict with the legitimate interests of all the individuals at the level of their main employment: an example would be in a decision to redistribute the staff of one department among several other departments. Add to this the contribution that the rotation of membership may make to a committee's ability to monitor and learn from the effects of its early decisions and one could accept, without any imputation of individual integrity, the possibility of a high incidence of doubtful policy making.

Indeed the situation can be compounded by the natural inclination of committees to make decisions of principle without having to work through the detail of practical implications. This is a major factor which contributes to the degree of slippage between the conception and execution of a policy. On the other hand, a committee which shows a close concern with the detail of implementation may reveal its participants' legitimate interest in no policy being made at all rather than one which can be seen as deleterious to their interests in areas where their individual responsibility is clear. Thus academics tend to work in and contribute to a milieu in which a good deal of interpretation is possible in the carrying out of duties and in which uncertainty is endemic.

All organizations and institutions respond to stimuli, and a very powerful form of stimulus is the existence of management norms or models which are used within and between institutions. The academic objectives of an institution can easily be thwarted if staff conclude that resource allocation methods favour effort in other directions. The mechanical use of such norms as 'full-time-equivalent student', student/staff ratio, and unit costs can distort the pattern of programmes offered. Conversely, if the academic staff can develop and defend alternative techniques which are consonant with sound academic objectives, resource allocation can reinforce and sustain developments which might otherwise be prejudiced. This illustrates the importance of the participation of academic staff in the management process. In the absence of firm academic guidance norms, techniques may well be imposed which constitute disincentives to the implementation of agreed policies.

At the SRHE Leverhulme seminar at which this paper originally was presented there was a general belief expressed that the approach of staff to teaching in higher education is nothing like professional enough. Is this a dereliction which may be laid at the feet of academic staff or is it simply another consequence of the managerial mode? In the public view the main purpose of having universities, polytechnics and colleges — or at least the reason for having so many of them, is to teach people. The larger part of their funds is given to them for that express purpose; the amount given is directly related to the number of students enrolled. On the face of it one might expect skill in arranging courses and in teaching to be a necessary, even sufficient attribute to lead to promotion to the highest levels. In fact it is not so, especially in the universities. As we have seen, power and prestige largely go to those whose standing is high among the research community. This is despite the fact that nearly 70 per cent of university staff and a little over 70 per cent of polytechnic staff agree that promotion is too dependent on publication and too little on teaching (Halsey 1980). Halsey and Trow (1971) discovered that among university staff, 64 per cent had a primary interest in research. Interest in teaching, it seems, becomes more prevalent with age; whereas only 18 per cent of those under 25 have a primary interest in teaching 65 per cent of those over 60 do. The group which conspicuously does not become more interested in teaching are those who become professors. This leads to the irony that funds for improving teaching are, by and large, designated and dispersed by one group with a strong interest in research (professors husbanding the prestige of their departments) and principally spent on training for the other group with the strongest involvement in research (the junior staff trying to establish themselves). It seems unlikely that efforts to train staff will have any significant effect until excellence in teaching is recognized and rewarded. In turn, that is unlikely to happen in organizations where the responsibility and rewards for research are attributable to individuals but the responsibility for teaching is attributable to a committee. The fact that staff training is more evident in the polytechnics and colleges than in the universities does not reflect a greater need for it in polytechnics; it reflects a system whose members are less secure in their attainment and retention of professional prestige and a job for life.

Areas of Discretion
In common with their colleagues in all European countries the academic staff of both universities and (so far as degrees are concerned) the public sector have full discretion in deciding the subjects they will teach, the topics they will include in those subjects, the relative emphasis they will give those topics and the teaching and examination regime they will create in association with their subject. Occasionally, very great freedom can be given to individuals even at a junior level, though all this is done within the context of mechanisms by which the profession regulates itself (faculty committees, external examiners, CNAA panels). One area of discretion which differentiates the British academic from his European colleagues is the complete freedom departments have to select or reject students without being required to give reasons for doing so, either within the institutions or publicly. This contrasts with educational policy in countries such as Denmark, Germany and the Netherlands in which all people who are qualified according to a national minimum standard have the right to enter university if they so wish. There are other more general freedoms. The university academic is a member of the university rather than an employee of it; and even in the public sector, where teaching staff are employed by the local authority, they are still regarded within the organization on much the same basis as a professional, such as a doctor. This contrasts with the Federal Republic of Germany and the Netherlands where university academic staff are civil servants and are bound by the conventions of that service. In the FDR the final decision on the appointment of academic staff rests with the minister, who will make a selection from three candidates proffered by the university. It is not unknown for applications to be rejected on the grounds of a candidate's political activities. In this country, even where an individual's wish to place particular political slants on his teaching has been

curbed by colleagues, there is no doubt about the individual's right to continuing employment. There is no equivalent here of 'berufsverbot'.

Career Structures
University staff are slightly more likely to enter their jobs direct from university than their polytechnic counterparts (although it is less than 17 per cent), and are a little more likely to be middle class and have gone to a prestigious school. University staff are considerably more likely than their polytechnic equivalents to have had some connection with Oxbridge either as a student or a junior member of staff: roughly 32 per cent of university staff, but only 10 per cent of polytechnic staff, have an Oxbridge connection (Halsey 1982). The average working life of a teacher in higher education is forty years. At least until the recent freezing of posts about one in eight would leave the profession during the first three years, because many are on short-term contracts. Thereafter very small numbers leave annually. Unfortunately, the statistics given to the Universities' Statistical Record do not distinguish between academics on short-term appointments and those holding posts with a presumption of tenure. This leads to problems in planning. For example, in the present financial difficulties, short-term posts are the easiest to cut, but in many departments they provide the only opportunities to encourage staff mobility and to employ lively young staff.

Most promotions to senior grades (senior lecturer/professor) occur in the early 40s and about seven out of ten staff can expect to be promoted if they continue in the profession — although if they haven't made it by age 50 the chances are very much less. Up to 1971 a man with a first-class Honours degree was twice as likely to be promoted as one without, and an Oxbridge or London degree increases prospects by about two-thirds. Publication and mobility also help substantially (Williams, Blackstone and Metcalf 1974). In universities, at least, there is hardly any recruitment from outside the education system directly into the senior grades.

There is very little doubt that within the profession a job in a university is seen by most as preferable to one in the public sector. For instance, three-quarters of polytechnic staff would seriously consider transferring to a university at the same salary, and nearly half would consider doing so even if the salary dropped. In contrast, over half the university staff would not transfer across the binary line even at a higher salary. In fact the chances of polytechnic staff crossing the line are seen as very slim, only one in twenty see themselves as doing so, and presumably the actual number is less. A further indication of the perceived superiority of the universities is shown when both polytechnic and university staff are asked to nominate the best department in their subject. About 40 per cent of polytechnic staff chose Oxford, Cambridge or London. The next chose Manchester, UMIST or Edinburgh. No other university or any polytechnic was mentioned first by as much as 2 per cent of the thousand polytechnic staff who responded. The same staff were asked to name the post which they would regard as the highest achievement in their profession. Thirty-four per cent chose a polytechnic post, but 45 per cent chose a university post. (76 per cent of the university staff chose a university post and 0.5 per cent chose a polytechnic post.)

Problems Reported by Staff
At a meeting of eleven senior academics and administrators (including three pro-vice-chancellors) which met in 1972, the members were asked to write down the problems which they thought were uppermost in their university at the time. Forty-one problems were assembled. These could be seen as falling into three groups: structure and staff; planning; and the management of learning. The first group showed a concern for making the committee structure of universities work and for coping with the atomization of departments. The planning group fell into three sub-groups concerned respectively with: the problems of long-term planning; balancing the demand for courses against employment opportunities and the interests of academics (which included a group of problems concerned with continuing education); problems or resource allocation within institutions (including the closure of departments). The third group contained problems which reflected attempts to move from subject-centred to student-centred teaching and a growing desire for inter-institutional co-operation (Warren Piper and Glatter 1977). A similar survey taken today might reflect similar concerns. It seems likely that the deepening financial crisis has simply exacerbated the same problems rather than changed their nature.

A common enough procedure amongst those who run staff courses or undertake consultancy within education is to ask staff their opinion of why teaching or research is not better than it is. Typically the answers point more to aspects of the regime under which staff work which deny them the opportunity of doing as well as they might, rather than to a lack of ability or a lack of knowledge in how, say, to design courses or to teach. One might respond with Mandy Rice Davis and say 'Well, they would say that wouldn't they', but even the briefest investigation suggests that money directed solely at improving staff's ability to undertake their work is ill-spent if not accompanied by an equal concern for the opportunity our structures and procedures afford them for exercising their professional ability and the incentives which are implicit in our organizations and career structures.

Are Universities trying to have it Both Ways?
At a recent meeting, academics drawn from four European countries were asked to list the characteristics they thought typified the work of their countries' lecturers in higher education. It was a small, informal survey but nonetheless indicative, as each of those taking part was involved in the joint exercise of writing a comparative account of the duties and working conditions of staff in all EEC countries. The features about the UK system

which appeared most striking to those from overseas included the following:

a The great independence from rules shown by UK academics.
b The freedom employed in interpreting budget headings.
c The extent to which decisions are taken informally.
d The degree to which academic staff take responsibility for their students.
e The amount of small group teaching and personal contact between staff and students.
f The favourable staff/student ratios.
g The unpolitical nature of (particularly) the universities.

These features are characteristic of a system offering an exclusive form of education at a very high cost. We have noted others during this introduction. The favourable staff/student ratios, the freedom of academics to teach what and how they like (see Chapter 4, pp. 118 ff.), the way money is given on student numbers alone and quality taken on trust, the relatively weak identity lecturers have as teachers as opposed to being, say, engineers or classicists, and the irrelevance of skill in teaching reflected in the day-to-day procedures of our institutions are all matters which might be associated with élite education. The question must be asked whether it is realistic for the universities to try to retain these characteristics and the polytechnics to wish to emulate them, when, at the same time, they lay claim to be the nation's means of supplying mass post-school education.

The planning and control of higher education raises questions about some of the basic assumptions upon which higher education (and particularly university) institutions have developed — in particular their academic autonomy, and their freedom to determine internally the distribution of available resources. It also calls into question the freedom of students and prospective students to make unfettered choices. The loss or curtailment of these freedoms might be the price to be paid for a rational, cost-effective system. Would it be worth it?

THE NATIONAL CONTEXT

National Planning

The overall level of funding of higher education is a political decision, taken by government, and is related to total public expenditure. The proportion of the funding that is used for the support of staff is not laid down by any body, but is the result of policies at the micro-level. Nevertheless financial pressures have led to the employment of fewer staff in the past eight years than would have been expected from historical patterns. This is reflected in a worsening of the overall staff/student ratio. This was forecast to reach 1:10 by 1981 in the government white paper of 1972, *Education — A framework for Expansion*. Such ratios are not laid down nationally but are the result of competition for scarce resources.

The UGC policy of selectivity is necessary to give overall steer to the system and produce some macro-planning on a subject group basis. This permits each institution to have its own policies of resource allocation. There is, as yet, no comparable mechanism on the other side of the binary system.

In the public sector of higher education the regional advisory council/DES process of course approval does not involve any qualitative assessment of the ability of individual institutions to achieve a prescribed standard, nor has it involved any assessment of comparative costs. The system has been essentially one of planning by refusal. The machinery itself has not initiated proposals or shaped the provision. Inevitably pressure has been placed by ministers upon regional advisory councils and the Department of Education and Science to secure tighter control of the provision of advanced courses. For example, Further Education Circular 80/1 attempted to limit the freedom of the DES to approve new advanced courses by imposing a constraint that, for the time being, only those courses with 'a vocational objective' should be approved. Already the stricter conditions for course approvals have resulted in courses closing or not starting as a result of low recruitment. Inevitably such decisions have produced staffing problems within institutions. (It has also resulted in a less even distribution of courses than hitherto.)

No formal process has existed to ensure that joint planning takes place between the public and university sectors. Whilst the financial constraints being experienced by all institutions of higher education are forcing them to take account of what is going on in 'rival institutions', there is growing acceptance that a better mechanism to control the provision of courses across the binary line is overdue.

The UGC has acted in a dirigiste fashion in the planning of resources in a small number of highly expensive areas of which medicine is the most important example. In the protected period of the medical courses at Southampton, Nottingham and Leicester, grants were 'earmarked', and thus a base line provision for staff was incorporated. When the earmarking ended, these medical faculties had to argue their case for resources in the same way as the rest of their university. Another example is provided by law courses, for which the library costs are considerable. In practice the formation of new law departments was restricted to those where approval was notified and resources were provided. The case of considerable over-provision for Russian studies arose despite general warnings repeated over many years, and attention was focused on this when the UGC produced its report on Russian studies with its recommendation of concentration. In other cases UGC sub-committees have made recommendations to the main committee, which has resulted in formal approval of new courses when letters of guidance to institutions have been issued. This was a familiar procedure in quinquennial guidance. The guidance was not, however, finally prescriptive and in some cases universities adopted their own priorities within their financial constraints. In the situation of financial cutbacks and increased pressures, the guidance letters can be interpreted as course disapproval mechanisms.

From time to time bodies are set up to make recommendations about particular academic or professional areas, which reports are often highly productive and stimulating. Examples in recent years include that of the Finniston Committee, and reports on biotechnology. One feature, however, unites the bodies concerned: namely, that they have no funds to support their recommendations; and the issues are then resolved into the availability of money to carry out the innovations suggested. When government is unable to make special funds available, there is a taxing of the system by the UGC, if it is decided to implement the recommendations. It is always important that such innovatory proposals be costed and the source of finance indicated so that band-wagon jumping be minimized. It should be noticed that such planning thrusts for a supply of graduates for employment are subject to a long delay except when the courses required are one-year postgraduate courses. The tendency to forget the planning timetable can lead to delays of four or five years from the inception of a course to the production of graduates. Often this is far too long.

The Universities and the Role of the UGC
The present role of the UGC includes giving advice to individual universities and making financial allocations to universities which usually correspond to that advice. The UGC's other role is to offer advice to government and of necessity this advice is confidential. The powers of the UGC are therefore persuasive and financial.

Universities are independent chartered bodies and consequently can accept, modify or reject advice, but they do not have the power to alter the financial boundary conditions imposed upon them by the UGC. The strength of the UGC in this arrangement has been based upon the fact that, through its many sub-committees and its use of peer judgements its advice has usually been seen to be as disinterested as possible. This, however, is now subject to criticism, largely because the financial situation implies contraction rather than growth. The acceptance of the UGC and its directives may have been due to the fact that it was always in the position of providing funds for new developments. Not every development was accomplished, but at least some were, and the scale of continued growth gave confidence to universities as a whole.

The management of a system in contraction, or even in a steady state, is far more crucial and difficult than in expansion. Consequently it is of fundamental importance to the planning process that the UGC be given sufficient notice of the time-scale on which changes have to be introduced. The position in the last eight years shows the importance of this need. Nevertheless the UGC can only carry out what is feasible within the political and economic future. The previous assumptions of continued growth and increased prosperity are presumably no longer realistic and it is apparent that no government seems willing to make firm commitments for longer than one financial year at a time. The importance for universities of a longer time-scale is self-evident. The average student spends three or four years at college and consequently the time required to introduce and consolidate change is nearer to the old quinquennium and is certainly far greater than the one-year changes which have been required so frequently in the past few years.

It would therefore be premature to make suggestions about a totally new role for the UGC, or for giving the UGC some entirely different function, without consideration of the overall national political/economic dimension. If university charters remain as they are, then it remains the right of each university to formulate its academic policy and to pursue it with all the consequences which that implies for academic and other staff. The conflict between freedom and direction is not easily resolved.

The strength of the UGC lies in the confidentiality of its role. Universities can feel a relationship of trust because information which they give to the UGC is not given to any other body, and certainly not to the government. Similarly the government can trust the UGC because of the confidentiality of its advice to the government and of its relationship with ministers. If either of these areas of trust is broken, then the position of the UGC and the nature of the British university system is imperilled. It is important that this trust be preserved in the future. It should be noted that the UGC is in a state of continual interchange of information with the various bodies in the university sector, such as the Committee of Vice-Chancellors and Principals, the Association of University Teachers, the National Union of Students, campus unions and the research councils. At the same time it is in a state of interplay with the Department of Education and Science, the Scottish Education Department and the Welsh Office. It is important that any suggestions for change retain the benefits of the present system.

The UGC has traditionally carried out this role for the universities primarily through its major quinquennial exercises. The last quinquennium (1972-7) was a victim of the economic crisis of 1973/4 and since that time we have had, variously, annual financing, the rolling triennium of the Labour administration with a numbers target for 1981/2, the steady state of 79/80 coupled with the three scenarios (A,B and C), and now the cuts extending from 82/2 to 83/4.

The overall picture of rapidly changing plans has made staff planning very difficult indeed. The changing scene has not created confidence and the lack of any sustained horizon for the past eight years, coupled with the demographic projections into the next decade, create a feeling of alarming uncertainty.

There is a need for increasing co-operation and co-ordination across the binary line. The lack of adequate trans-binary planning exacerbates the difficulties and the lack of overall planning mechanisms in the public sector means that the UGC has no corresponding partner for detailed co-ordinative purposes. There is at present no means of ensuring that a contraction of a particular provision in the university sector will not result in a growth of provision for the same area in the public sector.

In trans-binary planning there is a need to take due financial account of the importance of the universities in fundamental scientific research and for this to be reflected in the financial baselines. If this is ignored the staffing resource will be affected. The research contribution of university staff is fundamental to sustaining the national research activity, concentrated as the major part of this is in the universities. The national planning area thus embraces the research councils in addition to the UGC and the variety of bodies involved in the public sector. The dual support system of research is vital to national planning: it is under severe stress at the present time.

Public Sector Higher Education
In the UK public sector higher education is administered by four agencies: the Scottish Education Department, the Welsh Office, the Northern Irish Office and the Department of Education and Science. This contrasts strongly with the unified responsibility of the UGC for all the universities in Great Britain. Up to now institutions in the public sector of higher education have had no national reference point for guidance or advice as to which reductions in the curriculum might be appropriate. The lack of considered advice from the centre can result in the reduction or elimination of courses in accordance with no national plan, but simply as a result of local decisions.

The DES says of the interim National Advisory Body recently set up:

> 'Whatever form of new national body might be established in the public sector of higher education, two years at least will elapse before any such body could begin to influence the system. In the meantime, resource constraint and the beginning of the decline in the eighteen year old age group will be forcing changes on the system (indeed, are already forcing such changes) with the clear risk that they will be largely unco-ordinated, causing damage to national provision as a result. This applies both within the public sector of higher education and as between that and the university sector. Ministers are, therefore, resolved that priority attention should turn to identifying what immediate steps are possible to achieve co-ordinated change within and between the sectors of higher education, to come into operation at the earliest opportunity.'

It is clear that the primary objective of the interim, and subsequently of any permanent, national body is to create coherent arrangements for the planning and control of courses in public sector higher education, to establish with the UGC effective methods to ensure joint planning and distribution in the provision of courses, to effect a more equitable means of distributing monies for the funding of institutions, and to promote innovation in the institutions as a result of government advice. All this must be achieved within the overall climate of a sharp reduction in resources for higher education.

The principal issues that will be faced by the national body arise from the facts that (i) some 380 institutions currently provide advanced further education courses, (ii) the principal providers of public sector higher education comprise about 90 institutions (ie the polytechnics, the colleges and institutes of higher education) and 24 institutions not under the control of local education authorities, controlled by voluntary bodies and funded by direct grants from the DES. This heterogeneous collection of institutions, within and between which there is now duplication of provision, evolved to meet quite different needs from those of today. The new national advisory body (NAB) for public sector higher education will have to begin the job of deciding who should do what — what the roles and objectives of institutions should be. Implicit in this are judgements of academic quality; the methods used to make these judgements will have to withstand public scrutiny.

Trans-binary Issues

The institutions of higher education in the public sector, together with the universities, offer programmes of a similar standard and jointly seek to meet the demand for undergraduate and postgraduate education in the UK. The fact that 55 per cent of the provision is administered by the universities and 45 per cent by public sector higher education institutions poses problems about the national allocation of resources for higher education. For example:

    i   The distribution of courses between institutions across the binary line.
    ii   The provision of monies to the institutions.

There is no national scheme whereby all courses in the same geographical or subject area are assessed by a single agency before approval is given. There are significant differences in the levels of funding of universities courses and of non-university institutions. There is evidence that teaching staff in public sector higher education institutions undertake more hours of teaching than their university counterparts; this may mean that they undertake less research and/or consultancy. Many of them feel that the lower level of provision prejudices their ability to maintain standards and keep their curricula up to date. They fear that they would be less likely to secure support for the continuance of their work if a choice had to be made between their institution and a university.

The case for trans-binary planning of course distribution and the allocation of finance has become more urgent as a consequence of cuts in allocations to both the UGC and the Pool for Advanced Further Education. It also raises questions about the unit costs in the two sectors.

Institutional Freedom and National Planning
The essence of academic freedom is the right of an institution of higher education to determine which courses it will offer, and of the individual teachers of that institution to determine the nature of the syllabuses and the way they will be taught, without reference to a superior authority. Such an absolute concept is untenable if there is to be a policy of national direction and control. No such absolute concepts have been held in public sector higher education institutions because they generally have to obtain support for their courses from their maintaining local education authority. Furthermore all courses have to have the approval of the Department of Education and Science. Hence there is double accountability (see Chapter 3, pp. 107 ff. and Chapter 4, pp. 131 ff.). The type of detailed course control in public sector higher education institutions outlined above does not exist in the universities. Whilst the University Grants Committee allocates finance and issues broad guidelines to universities, the UGC has no mandatory authority to prescribe the courses of an individual university.

National planning has to be related to institutional freedom. The best national planning calls for interactive procedures. To be effective these require more time for decision making than has been normal in recent years. Universities are often ambivalent about this interaction. Some academics wish the UGC to intervene to protect their own individual discipline and interests when these are threatened by their colleagues, but object strenuously when the UGC threatens their interests by suggesting contraction or cessation of activity. This suggests that the present balance between intervention and institutional freedom is about right. Freedom requires institutions to take responsible decisions, meaning that they must take the consequences of their bad decisions as well as the credit for their far-sighted ones.

A Local Regional Role
The inter-dependence of the full-time and part-time courses is crucial to the local/regional role of public sector higher education institutions. Their origins mostly lie in the provision of part-time programmes of higher education for a wide range of locally-based students, who were generally older than the traditional full-time students, and may have included graduates needing post-experience training/education. Such origins have given these institutions strong local and regional roots. Today much advanced part-time work in the public sector exists under the umbrella of equivalent full-time courses provided to students from a much wider geographical area. The fact that most public sector higher education institutions are funded in the first instance by the local education authorities

and have governing bodies composed of men and women with strong local/regional connections, results in policies with a strong local/regional orientation and ethos.

Local education authorities can all too easily alienate academic staff. First, it often happens that the academic strength of a part-time course is dependent upon a parallel full-time course which sustains a cadre of staff of sufficient quality who will also engage in teaching on the part-time programme. Considerations of unit costs, student numbers and fee income are leading some institutions to examine the balance between full, part-time and evening study, and the feasibility of arrangements for students to qualify at all levels by combinations of all three types of study. Part-time and evening courses are rarely prestigious. Such changes could raise problems for those teachers who have had a long association with more traditional modes of study, and their implementation will demand sensitivity and skill.

Furthermore, the local ethos for part-time courses may be financially disadvantageous for the institution. If, because of different levels of fees and inappropriate methods of calculating unit costs, part-time study is made to seem more expensive than the full-time, institutions are tempted to achieve economies at the expense of part-time students.

Thirdly, we have seen that institutions in the public sector of higher education usually agree their curricula with the local authority (and in some cases have to). Not only does this conflict with desires of institutional autonomy and individual freedom in academic affairs, but such a process embraces an element of planning, and there is no mechanism by which the local authority, development corporation, industrial and commercial planners, etc., can, together with the institutions, seek to establish the need for courses and plan to meet the need. Most course provision is on an ad hoc basis and results from the efforts of teaching staff to liaise with industry, commerce and other interests. It is less common for those who are planning change in the community to recognize the need to involve institutions of higher education (and of FE) in securing the training of personnel. Some public sector institutions maintain advisory committees, which operate under the aegis of the governing bodies, whose function is to feed information into the institution relevant to the planning of the curricula.

The local impact of universities mostly relates to post-experience courses and continuing professional education. The local/regional inputs for these often come through departments rather than the institution as a whole. This is an area for which encouragement is being given nationally.

SUMMARY AND PROPOSALS

THE INDIVIDUAL STAFF MEMBER

Countering the Skewed Age Structure

Proposition 1.01 The age structure of the profession, thanks to the expansion of the 1960s and early 1970s, is not such as to facilitate a run-down by normal retirements. Rather it is such as to lead to the severe frustration of career aspirations in middle life owing to the paucity of senior vacancies in the next few years. It should be a major object of the national policies to tackle this skewed age structure; merely to facilitate the retirement of older staff by a few years will not meet the morale and professional problems of the teaching force. Some measures to encourage people in early and mid-life to change their careers, either within or preferably outside the teaching profession, should be considered. Too much reliance on early retirement as a means of adjusting staff levels does not tackle the fundamental problem of the skewed age structure. Unless more is done, problems of a different kind will emerge later. Almost certainly, financial incentives need to be considered now as the cost later could be far greater.

Flexibility in Employment

Proposition 1.02 As the higher education system adjusts itself to severely straightened circumstances, and adapts to the changing and developing needs of society, it will need the greatest flexibility of teacher employment consonant with the maintenance of standards and the professional satisfaction of staff of the required calibre. The need is for mobility to be much greater between the education system and industrial and commercial employment. As a short-term response to the current crisis one might consider a kind of labour exchange, where industry and employers can contact academics, initially for short-term release. Industry would gain by having highly qualified people in certain fields to meet short-term needs and the academic staff would benefit from increased industrial experience.

Proposition 1.03 If flexibility of career pattern is to be achieved, attention must be paid by government to rigidities and disincentives arising from the disadvantages of transferring between pension and superannuation schemes; this is a particular problem when transfer into, or out of, the private employment sector is involved, but it can also impede movement between the higher education sectors.

Proposition 1.04 The required flexibility for such innovations could only be obtained with considerable modification of the current tenure conventions. One possibility would be for teachers to hold tenure in the system rather than in an individual institution; if the binary divide is too deep to permit this in one step, then at least let the principle apply on each side. Sharing of staff already occurs, usually in relation to specialist and minority subjects; the proposal is to generalize this arrangement.

Proposition 1.05 Sharing of staff across the binary division is impeded by the different and separately negotiated salary scales on the two sides, as well as by pension scheme differences, etc. That the scales are separate is inevitable under the present divided system, and merging of the two sectors merely for administrative tidiness and convenience would be not only educationally wrong but would prejudice the special functions of institutions on each side of the line. But some correspondence could be adopted in the names of levels of posts (eg lecturer). In addition, it should not be too difficult to arrange for at least some of the points on the salary scales to coincide, perhaps the top of the senior lecturer scale in the public sector and the lecturer scale in the universities. Perhaps also there is a case for the abandonment of the principal lecturer grade or for renaming it so that the top of the teaching profession in the public sector corresponds with the top of the professorial range in universities. At the moment it is noticeable that only the top directorate posts in the public sector have salaries comparable to those in the professorial range of universities. We are attracted by the formula adopted in the universities for determining professorial salaries. There is a national minimum salary and a mean: each institution is free to offer whatever salaries it wishes above the minimum provided that the mean of all professorial staff does not exceed the agreed figure. With such changes it would still be possible for differing institutional roles to be recognized by varying the proportion of senior staff.

Proposition 1.06 Salary scales for teachers in higher education should include bars or blocks, progression beyond which would be conditional upon evidence of satisfactory performance as judged by publicly declared criteria. Where such barriers have existed up to now they have either been used so sparingly as to cast doubts on the value of the exercise or (in public sector higher education) they have been undermined by the negotiation of automatic progression entitlements and scale-transfers. In general we are in favour of bars and blocks being maintained and becoming important decision points. We would recommend this strengthening of the current system if the modification of the tenure rules recommended below do not find favour.

Proposition 1.07 There is need for nationally agreed criteria for the holding of tenure. The present wide variation between the sectors and between institutions produces anomalies and inhibits the process of rationalization which the pressure on resources is making more urgent. Currently the United Kingdom is unique in Europe in offering tenure at such an early stage in an academic career.

Proposition 1.08 Any modifications of the terms of tenure would have to be nationally negotiated and this would no doubt be a lengthy and difficult process. The present models of tenure might be appropriate for universities if they reverted to being exclusive, specialist institutions dedicated to quality, with a small proportion of the country's students and a small proportion of the educational budget; but the present models of tenure are not serving the best interests of the higher education system as a whole. The entrenchment of an individual, at a relatively early age, does not correspond to the needs of an institution whose first duty is the maintenance of the standards of the teaching it provides. Nor does it necessarily correspond with the best interests of an individual or the statistical expectations of professional development. It inhibits career change, reduces incentives to refreshment and re-training, and encourages institutional introversion. In future tenure should not be granted as early as it has been and the form of tenure actually granted should be carefully qualified.

Proposition 1.09 A number of variations on the tenure model can be envisaged. One might be for initial appointments to be made for a probationary period of, say, five years, followed by a fixed term contract of, say, seven years. Only at this point would the offer of a tenured post be considered, depending upon the satisfactory performance of the person concerned. A second model would be a probationary period followed by a ten year 'tenure' after which one of a number of options might follow. The individual could be offered tenure to retirement age, or tenure subject to a quinquennial review of performance, or a fixed-term contract after which tenure would be reconsidered, or employment with no tenure but subject to one year's notice. A third approach might be to effect a 'tapering' of tenure under which year by year the number of weeks covered by the basic salary would be gradually reduced for all staff; this process might take five or six years, by which time staff would have ten to twelve weeks per year in which they were free to take other employment within or outside their own institutions.

Proposition 1.10 An alternative to modifications to the terms of tenure would be to change the conditions of service so that the (reduced) salary paid would be in respect of a basic teaching commitment which would in itself not constitute a whole-time programme; it would be possible for staff to augment this basic salary with short-term or limited tenure posts held in the same or another institution. The second job could vary greatly and in this way staff could experiment, gain experience and confidence, and develop expertise outside their teaching specialism.

Proposition 1.11 The contribution of part-time teachers, including those from industry holding associate posts, has always been valued but the numbers have generally been relatively small. An increase in the proportion of such appointments would not only add flexibility but would strengthen the links between higher education and industry and commerce. The involvement of practitioners in professional education varies for no apparent reason other than historical accident. In architecture and medicine for instance it is accepted that there are many part-time appointments. This is less true in engineering. In teacher training it does not happen at all; and teacher training is the worse for it. Again, in medicine the top practitioners play a crucial role, in the final year of qualification. To some extent that is true in architecture, but it is not true in engineering or the chemical industries or law. We regard the involvement of senior people from the professions as highly desirable and some mechanism should be produced to make such arrangements not only possible, but as normal a part of professional education as it is in medicine.

Proposition 1.12 A variant on part-time employment could be the voluntary reduction of commitment by the employee from full-time to (say) three or four days per week, with proportional reduction in salary and responsibility, on the understanding that such jobs would then be preferentially protected if redundancies occurred; employees would be able to buy back full pension rights, and would be free to take other employment.

Proposition 1.13 The extension of a reliance on part-time teachers cannot be achieved without overcoming some problems. It is often the part-time appointments which are the first to be terminated in times of recession (although currently those part-timers who have been lost seem set to be replaced by former full-timers induced to take early retirement and then employed back at reduced salaries on a part-time basis). The flexibility of part-timers is both their weakness and their strength. The flexibility of their appointment allows them to be easily dismissed; but the flexibility of their working lives enables the institution to use them in responding to changing and uncertain circumstances. It must also be recognized that trade unions are likely to resist the employment of part-time staff if it appears to represent a switching of resources away from full-time posts. Nonetheless, we believe these problems should be addressed rather than avoided.

Proposition 1.14 By contrast, we suspect that the current position is that entitlements to sabbatical leave are often not taken up. We should like to see some facts on this point collected and published. One of the effects of extreme pressure upon resources is to make the system of sabbatical leave vulnerable. Not only are institutions tempted to curtail the opportunity, but teachers to whom such leave is due may feel disinclined to take it in full, knowing the pressures under which their colleagues would be working. It is important that the system is sustained, especially if the terms of tenure are modified, so that staff have the opportunity for professional development, refreshment and research. Indeed there is a strong case for widening the scope of the scheme to include systematic retraining or preparation for career change.

Proposition 1.15 In connection with widening the use to which sabbatical leave is made, we should like to see more frequent secondments and exchanges of staff. Institutions have a wide variety of regulations governing these matters. We believe that on the whole they could do with attention, not only to make the movement of staff more easy, but also to protect the interests of the staff who avail themselves of opportunities. We suspect that encouragement is particularly needed for staff who feel they may lose their place in the promotion queue or who fear their institution would find it did not miss their erstwhile contribution. We also believe there should be much more international mobility of staff. This is particularly so within the European Community where attempts are being made to increase compatibility in professional training between countries. It has sadly to be recognized that, because the British are frequently deficient in languages, it is often easier for overseas staff to come here than for British academics to take posts in another country. However, a number of European countries, notably Holland and Denmark and the Scandinavian countries, often accommodate courses taught in English.

Proposition 1.16 One of the assumptions in encouraging the mobility of staff is that the curriculum exists independently of the teacher. In practice, this is not always so, particularly in the universities, where the ideal of academic freedom extends to individual teachers having considerable discretion over the content and form of their courses. This is another example of the ideals of university education conflicting with arrangements which seem sensible for the mainstream of post-school education.

Proposition 1.17 Incentives should be devised and developed for teaching staff to seek secondment to other jobs for periods of six months or a year at a time. Incentives could include the continuance of a proportion of basic salary plus full superannuation contributions and the demonstration that such secondments are positive factors when promotion is under consideration. Not only would this refresh and enliven the teaching programme and ensure its relevance to conditions outside academe, but it would facilitate the kind of career mobility which is desirable by revealing the occasional unexpected opportunity.

Proposition 1.18 The determination of sharing/transfer arrangements between institutions is not only administratively complex, it involves academic sensitivities and affects careers. It must be done with care, with full and open consultation, and with the interests of students as well as of staff in mind; but it will have to be faced with resolution.

Proposition 1.19 Management functions within institutions are best discharged by those who are, or recently have been active academics; there is much to be said against permanent appointments to management posts. Good teachers and researchers are more likely to be willing to undertake administrative and managerial responsibilities if they are ensured of a right of return to their academic work. This flexibility is at present possible (though not always invoked) in the universities but is absent in the public sector, where life appointments to senior management posts are the rule. It should be possible in all institutions for senior management posts to be held on limited tenure, with full rights of return, with appropriate salary adjustment.

Proposition 1.20 In the public sector the Burnham negotiating machinery has over the years appeared to give special weight to administrative duties carried out by teaching staff to the extent that appointment to senior posts within the teaching grades is seen as automatically involving a reduction in teaching and an increase in administration. Students should not be deprived of good teachers who have been deemed worthy of promotion, and it is doubtful whether paying teachers more to teach less and do more administration is a good use of money.

Proposition 1.21 There should also be the possibility of enhanced progression up salary scales in recognition of exceptional merit, again in accordance with publicly declared criteria and nationally agreed rules.

Staff Development

Proposition 1.22 The practice of regular staff development reviews, common in most large public and private organizations, should become universal in higher education. Ideally such reviews should be annual and they should be distinguished from promotion exercises. The format and procedure for such reviews should be determined in consultation with staff, and the main object of each review would be to assist the member of staff concerned in his professional and career development (See Chapter 2, pages 79 ff.).

Proposition 1.23 Since promotion to senior posts is going to be a slow and difficult process for some years to come, the question of some way of recognizing the professional merit of good teachers should be faced. The use of conventional professorial titles is one way of doing this (perhaps extended to, for example, associate or assistant professor); another would be the more or less public process of peer and student evaluation leading to honorary awards or titles (cf. Chapter 4, pages 80 ff.).

Proposition 1.24 All institutions in higher education should be prepared to invest a larger proportion of their resources in staff training and development. Apart from the irony of institutions devoted to learning being so reluctant to help their staff learn more of the job they are employed to do, higher education compares very badly indeed with other public bodies such as the civil service and the health service. The British civil service provides some 1,000 places each year on ten-week courses for principal grade civil cervants alone; yet 90 per cent of the civil service training is provided within departments rather than on courses. The hospital service provides management training for administrative, medical, scientific and technical staff. The number of places on management courses for nurses alone has been estimated at 12,000 per annum (Leggatt 1972).

A modest beginning might be for it to be agreed on both sides of the binary line how much time might be reasonable to allow for staff release for training. Even something as minimal as a mean of one week per year would be a considerable advance on the present position (cf Chapter 2, page 94).

Proposition 1.25 Whatever the unit of structure, responsibities must be assigned within it and among them will be those for the management of resources in general and academic staff in particular. Hitherto little has been done in the university sector to prepare people to discharge such responsibilities. The Further Education Staff College, valuable though its work is, does not have the capacity to do all that is needed to train management in the public sector. More serious attention should be given to this problem. A small fraction of the expenditure on the whole system should be made available explicitly for the development of management expertise in senior staff.

THE INSTITUTIONAL SETTING

Organizational Developments

Proposition 2.01 The overall outlook for higher education is one of contraction; for the staff this must constitute a threat, since most estimates of the rate of retrenchment are considerably higher than any process of natural wastage. Leaving aside, for the moment, the effect on staff themselves, one of the principal and most pervasive effects of resource constraints will be that student/staff ratios will be less favourable. If staff/student ratios rise, will the student experience suffer? There is a lack of research and even of empirical evidence on the relationship, if any, between staff/student ratios, the maintenance of academic standards and the satisfaction of student needs. A pilot-scheme should be commissioned in this area, to guide policy and to help teachers to cope with the problems. Among the factors to be considered, the effect of the teaching staff/support staff ratios upon unit costs and upon educational efficiency is one of the more important. How do we accommodate to changing staff/student ratios? It is not just a matter of staff working longer hours or doing more in the way that they have always done it. There must be changes of strategy, approach and method, which inevitably will affect the quality, though not necessarily the overall value, of the education on offer. All this needs to be investigated.

Proposition 2.02 Subject to the moderating effect of peer evaluation, academic staff have been accustomed to develop curricula largely around their own academic interests. Current uncertainties and resource constraints are likely to freeze the curriculum as staff shrink from innovation. Precisely at the time when the system should be most open to change staff feel threatened, and react by concentrating on the tasks in hand, particularly those which are apparently most in demand. Some flexibility in funding is needed if innovation is to be encouraged; should a proportion of any savings made by staff redundancies be returned to the teaching departments for educational innovation?

Proposition 2.03 The proportion of institutional funds devoted to monitoring the performance of institutions and to system maintenance is, we suggest, disastrously low. The systematic and professional collection of management data which might inform policy making should be a feature of all institutions. There is much to be said for a specialist unit taking on this function or for it to be combined with a staff development unit.

Proposition 2.04 Within institutions, and between institutions, comparisons of unit costs for similar activities are now commonplace. It is important to recognize that the mode of analysis which is employed (assuming it is publicly known, as it should be) will itself react upon the academic process. Staff will be under strong incentives to modify practices to give more favourable figures, and these modifications may not be educationally desirable. In selecting methods of analysis, therefore, teachers should be involved who are alert to these effects. The present approach using the concept of a 'full-time-equivalent' student concept is an example. Especially in the public sector the weighting discourages part-time courses. 'Management information' about the use of resources should be widely disseminated and clearly interpreted.

Proposition 2.05 The vitality of teaching and of research will inevitably suffer if there is no young intake into the higher education teaching profession; in the short term national policies are unlikely to give a positive lead, but local initiatives could make some impression by negotiating sponsored short-term engagements specifically for young scholars and teachers. As we have observed earlier, in the long term the health of the teaching function depends upon a reasonably balanced age structure for the profession. The room for manoeuvre required by an institution which is to keep control of its own development cannot be attained by minimizing redundancy and early retirement. The ability to continue to make some new appointments is an essential part of a realistic strategy to fit an institution to its future work. A tough management policy of this kind is possibly easier in the public sector than in the universities where the management structure is primarily geared to the protection of those comprising the current collegium.

Proposition 2.06 Throughout higher education, but especially in non-university institutions where research traditions are less strongly rooted, the effect of resource constraints and emphasis upon staff/student ratios and class sizes is putting ever greater pressure upon staff to increase their teaching commitment at the expense of research, even that which is externally funded. Even so, it should be remembered that polytechnic staff are competing in the same labour market as staff from universities; their career chances, as much as those of their university colleagues, depend upon the quality and extent of their research. Recognition that research is a legitimate and esteemed activity is in itself not enough (though it is a necessary first step in many institutions); some protection must be given to those whose research competence is proven, so that in unit cost exercises the contribution of (and cost of) their research is realistically allowed for. In the long run, the effect of the pressure on staff/student ratios and class sizes is likely to affect the quality of teaching and the morale of staff, who find a conflict between the immediate requirements of their employment and the best interests of their career chances.

Proposition 2.07 The tradition in universities and to a lesser extent in other institutions is for staff to be encouraged to develop academic specialisms; they naturally seek every way to enhance their particular expertise. The teaching of basic courses to first-year students or to students majoring in other disciplines is not an attractive occupation to them. Yet these groups need good teachers, more than those who are more mature and more strongly motivated. Is there a case for the generalist or general-purpose teacher of basics in each area? — a teacher who takes his pedagogic responsibilities seriously and devotes himself to the needs of these particular categories. Can pedagogic expertise compensate for the loss of immediacy which may be the result of such teachers not being research specialists?

Proposition 2.08 The oft repeated claim that research strengthens teaching loses some of its force when it is found, as it is in some departments, that there is no, or a negative, correlation between those who do the research and those who do the undergraduate teaching. It is a corollary of this claim that such teachers might well do more contact teaching than their colleagues. We, on the other hand, wish to make a distinction between an argument which says that individual teachers should all be involved in research and one that says that teaching should be undertaken in a department which is involved in research.

Proposition 2.09 Contraction requires innovation if it is to be manned successfully. Yet contraction is unfavourable to innovation when it encourages staff to cling to well-tried and hitherto well-supported programmes. Yet such a reaction can only have deleterious effects on the education system. One major cause of the reluctance to innovate is the general lack of shared models of how educational institutions work. Because we lack such models and the institutional monitoring units which might develop them, major policy decisions are in danger of being made by force majeur. Is there a case for taxing the whole of the higher education system to provide a fund for institutions or departments to support specific innovations and to develop ways to monitor styles of educational managements?

Proposition 2.10 Management styles and emphasis on cost-effectiveness can adversely affect the quality of teaching; at the extreme, cramming hundreds of students into lecture rooms when there are no resources for their adequate tutorial supervision would be a negation of the academic standards built up over the years. The teachers in higher education are, as a profession, proud of those standards and committed to maintaining them; they must be the watch-dogs. Institutions must be prepared to forego the financial advantages of an increased intake if this is bought at the expense of lower standards. This is not to say that the maintenance of high standards with a worsening staff/student ratio cannot be achieved with careful attention to teaching strategies and methods.

Proposition 2.11 The department is the commonest unit of organization within institutions; by and large it is subject-based and provides a base or home for students who identify with it and staff who work in it. It provides a structure to which staff can relate, and which is more or less hierarchical according to local determination. While the defects of departmental units are well known, schemes which avoid the tribal frontiers and territorial exclusiveness of departments — those invoking matrix structures, for example — do not provide clear management and decision-making structures and are not well adapted to deciding priorities in times of retrenchment. Such considerations, as well as arguments based upon the economy of size, suggest that large multi-subject groupings will become common; as a result staff may well see their horizons or scope of activity widened, but may lose their sense of identification.

Proposition 2.12 Institutions should be given clear targets on realistic time-scales so that staff can plan accordingly. Uncertainty about future funding reflects back on individual members of staff who adopt defensive postures, identify with what are thought to be safe options and lose interest in innovation because of the inherent element of uncertainty. This is a recipe for academic stagnation and introversion, and for sterile in-fighting.

Proposition 2.13 Debates about priorities and planning involve discussions of criteria by which the viability of activities are to be judged. Some greater element of discrimination and specialization between institutions seems inevitable. When deciding which areas of work institutions should seek to share or shed, the criteria should not only be cost-effectiveness, but should take account of the concept of 'critical mass', or size of unit, below which interchange of ideas and balance of interests are likely to be inadequate for scholarship. The first remedy to be sought is the sharing or pooling of specialist or minority subject interests, in the hope that strong viable units will be formed or will develop.

Proposition 2.14 The processes of peer evaluation are widely acknowledged in higher education — indeed the whole concept of academic standards depends upon them. Hitherto they have been used to determine criteria and priorities for growth, promotion and development. In the future they will be used to decide criteria and priorities for closures, redundancies and transfers. In the interests of the survival of a reputable higher education system, staff must accept their role in the peer evaluation process, whatever pain and distress this causes and however difficult and arduous it is.

Proposition 2.15 The criterion by which courses should be retained or closed should not be a simplistic view of the employment prospects of graduates. The task of providing appropriate numbers of highly qualified personnel is only one function of the higher education system. It also provides opportunities for people to pursue their interests and to increase their chances of social mobility. A third function is to pass on from one generation to the next certain aspects of our culture including the theory of high technology as well as the embodiment of the well-rounded 'whole person'. The maintenance of national and international culture requires a balance between these three sometimes competing purposes; emphases may change from time to time, but should not be pushed too far by crude views of manpower needs. Similarly, the opinions of students should be considered relevant though not necessarily decisive. The academic community as a whole needs to be sensible to the fickleness of such criteria.

The Use of Resources

Proposition 2.16 It may be that if the teaching year could be restructured and the length of teachers' contracts changed, there could be a better use of plant and accommodation and an increase in the output of students. Institutions of higher education have an effective teaching year of thirty weeks. In institutions where little research is done most classrooms, laboratories and workshops are out of use for about two-fifths of the year and library facilities are also significantly under-used.

Proposition 2.17 If the teaching year were to be replanned, say on a basis of two fourteen-week semesters, it would be possible with re-adjusted course arrangements to have two additional eight-week or one additional fourteen-week teaching period which could allow (a) existing students to accelerate the completion of their course and (b) other additional students to undertake study whilst preserving employment for most of the year. Such arrangements might allow students to plan a combination of normal and exceptional periods of study.

Proposition 2.18 If staff contracts could be re-negotiated so that their teaching commitment were reduced by, say, six weeks per year, it would create the possibility for institutions to hire staff on an ad hoc basis for the additional sessions. Such an arrangement would allow teaching staff to gain experience of teaching in other institutions, provide the institutions with an opportunity of sampling staff who they may subsequently wish to employ permanently, create opportunities for students to vary their mode of tuition, and maximize the use of residential, teaching and library accommodation.

Proposition 2.19 It has been argued that any lengthening of the teaching year in institutions of higher education would reduce their research capacity. The use of 'summer sessions' is very common indeed in North American universities and the most prestigious of these offer major summer programmes. There seems to be little evidence that the research capacity of these institutions has waned as a result, and indeed there is evidence to the contrary.

Proposition 2.20 One of the principal advantages that might accrue from an extension of the teaching year would be that some students would wish to accelerate their courses by working and studying at times when otherwise they would take holidays or employment. With increasing pressure on the size of student grants in the UK it may be desirable to provide an opportunity for students to advance their final examination date and thereby reduce the financial burdens that result from an extended period of study.

Proposition 2.21 A reduction in the contractual teaching year for staff would only bring benefits if there were a concomitant reduction in the salaries of staff. A reduction in salaries would give rise to opportunities for other staff to be hired for the additional summer periods. (Extra income from tuition fees would also be attracted from students undertaking additional summer sessions.)

Proposition 2.22 The counter-arguments to these proposals maintain that to expand the teaching year is not in itself a better use of resources; it is a waste of a scarce resource, namely, the research capacity of the university system. In a country where a significant proportion of the research activity is concentrated in universities it would be a prodigal waste of this resource to diminish the opportunities for its exercise. There may well be scope for greater co-ordination in the use of resources by providing certain types of facility in carefully chosen centres. Scholars in the arts are used to travelling to certain libraries to pursue their research. This is also true of work in high energy physics. There may be other areas where this can be extended. Within urban areas co-ordination of library purchases and sharing of facilities may enable important journal subscriptions to be maintained. Policies for these economies should be developed by those who will have to exercise them in practice. This is far preferable to an imposed national scheme and is more likely to succeed with local initiative. Policies are best fostered by creating the climate of opinion to enable them to be exercised and developed. The present crisis may well produce more imaginative proposals to deal with our difficulties.

THE NATIONAL CONTEXT

National Planning

Proposition 3.01 To the extent that there is little publicly determined planning of higher education — none at all in the public sector — the work of staff is adversely affected. Not only is this a question of morale, it affects the efficiency of higher education's most costly resource — its teaching staff.

Proposition 3.02 It is of first importance to staff when deciding the overall shape and size of the higher education system, the role of institutions and the allocation of scarce resources, that matters of academic quality should be fully taken into account, and that the maintenance of academic standards should be a major objective. This will not happen if the system is at the mercy of short-term and emergency responses to financial pressures. Whatever the difficulties long- or at least medium-term planning must be facilitated.

Proposition 3.03 Rationalization of higher education, for whatever reasons it is undertaken, and whether or not it spans the binary division, is mainly a question of the disposition of staff — their terms and conditions of employment, their expertise, places of employment and career expectations.

Proposition 3.04 The work of staff is hampered and dissipated by the absence of well-defined and publicly known objectives for the institutions. Clear definition of the roles of institutions — universities, polytechnics and institutes of higher education — is a first requirement for the effective use of staff. 'Who does what?' is a matter of overall planning and control.

Proposition 3.05 Government determines the global resources available for higher education. On the university side of the binary line the UGC determines how its share shall be allocated; although some of its recent decisions have been criticized, as a mediator between institutions and central government its role is still generally defended. There is as yet no counterpart on the public sector side, though an interim body has just been set up jointly by the Council of Local Education Authorities and the DES. It is urgent that effective discussion should take place between UGC and a public sector body with similar responsibilities, otherwise duplication of staff effort and waste of resources are bound to occur.

The Need and Purpose of Research on Staff

Proposition 3.06 With a few exceptions, such as big science departments, the education system consists entirely of people helping other people learn and discover things. Seventy-four per cent of the higher education budget is for payroll expenditure. This includes national insurance, superannuation and all non-academic salaries. It follows that any adaption of the education system to changing circumstances or new purposes is primarily one of managing people. Of course financial management, resource allocation, the writing of regulations, the efficient use of plant and buildings all have a crucial importance; but they are not the primary means by which changes are brought about. The disciplines of economics, politics, law and policy studies, vital though they are, do not address themselves to the main issues when it comes to implementing rather than making, educational policy. What is needed, and will be ignored at great cost, are models of human interaction in both the seminar and the committee room, theories about teachers and educational organizations, and research on staff in all aspects of their work. The purpose of this is not that staff might be more easily controlled, for the value of the education system lies in the professional independence of its staff. What is required is the means and incentive for them to act corporately in the execution of national educational policy. This must be achieved without compromising their other great responsibility: that of undertaking free investigation and making disinterested comment. Academic staff occasionally need the licence to bite the hand that feeds them. That too is in the interests of humanity.

Proposition 3.07 For a profession committed (although in varying degrees) to research, higher education staff have done very little research on themselves, but there has been some work done on staff attitudes which would impinge on some of the suggestions made in this chapter. Some have been mentioned in the text, some other points are worth noting. On the matter of pay differences across the binary line, for instance, three-quarters of university staff think they should be paid more than polytechnic staff and even a quarter of polytechnic staff agree with them. On the slightly different question of whether there should be a common salary for university and polytechnic teachers, over 80 per cent of polytechnic teachers agree but 58 per cent of university teachers disagree. Interestingly, more polytechnic than university staff believe they should moderate demands for higher salaries, being already among the better paid members of the community: 55 per cent as opposed to 41 per cent.

Proposition 3.08 The chapter has emphasized our belief in the importance of training for higher education staff. The next chapter considers this issue in more detail. What little we know of people's commitment to the idea of teacher training suggests that the more senior the staff, the less their commitment, and that Scottish and Welsh universities are more favourably disposed than their English counterparts (Williams et al. 1974). In one Welsh university 63 per cent of staff thought that training should be provided (Startup 1979) which is not to say, of course, that they would find the time to attend any programme if it were arranged. Polytechnic staff on the whole seem more favourably disposed to teaching. Much more of this kind of information should be available. Indeed this, and very much more on people's attitudes to tenure, to departmental reorganization, to staff/student ratios, to mention but a few of those topics touched upon in this chapter, should be available as *a matter of course* at the institutional level; how else can institutions govern themselves on the democratic principles they all apparently espouse?

REFERENCES
ABRC and UGC (1982) *Report of a Joint Working Party on the Support of University Scientific Research* (Merrison Report) Cmnd. 8567

Halsey, A.H. and Trow, M.A. (1971) *The British Academics* London: Faber and Faber

Leggatt, T.W. (1972) *The Training of British Managers: a study of need and demand* Study conducted for the Institute of Manpower Studies commissioned by the Management Education Training and Development

Committee of the National Economic Development Office London: HMSO

Halsey, A.H. (1980) *Higher Education in Britain — A Study of University and Polytechnic Teachers* A Research Report to SSRC, March 1980

Halsey, A.H. (1982) The decline of donnish dominion? *Oxford Review of Education* April

Startup, R. (1979) *The University Teacher and his World* Farnborough: Saxon House

Williams, G., Blackstone, T. and Metcalf, D. (1974) *The Academic Labour Market* Amsterdam: Elsevier

2

THE PROFESSIONAL DEVELOPMENT OF TEACHING?

by Donald Bligh

The argument of this chapter is that the development of teaching is vital and possible, but difficult.

The arguments and the changes proposed are stated under the following propositions:

1.0 *The professional development of teaching needs to be planned.*
1.1 *Improvements are needed.*
1.2 *Changes are needed.*
1.3 *Policies and planning are needed.*
2.0 *Plans to change and improve teaching will need to be based upon methods shown to be feasible.*
2.1 *Acquisition of knowledge is needed.*
2.2 *Personal development is needed.*
2.3 *Practical skills are required.*
2.4 *Organizational development is needed.*
3.0 *Plans must obtain the commitment of social and working groups.*
3.1 *To be effective, professional development must be in accord with, or close to, the values of the basic social and working groups.*
3.2 *Basic social and working groups are, and will be, the main instruments of professional development.*
4.0 *The difficulties in implementing professional development plans need to be recognized at a senior level.*
4.1 *Basic social and working groups are, by their nature, resistant to change.*
4.2 *Professional development is easily perceived as a threat to an individual's self-esteem.*
4.3 *'Professional developers' themselves need professional development.*
4.4 *There is an inadequate basis of knowledge for professional development.*
4.5 *The development of teaching will be difficult while incentives seem to favour the development of research.*
5.0 *There is a need to institutionalize professional development.*
5.1 *There should be institutional policies for professional development.*
5.2 *To pursue professional development policies, institutions should make arrangements consonant with local circumstances.*
5.3 *Policies for professional development need to combine institutional authorization at the highest level with a personal sensitivity in*

their implementation.
- 5.4 *Institutional policies for professional development should include regular reviews of the aims and development of staff.*
- 5.5 *There should be systematic and formal procedures for the evaluation of teaching.*
- 5.6 *Senior staff, including heads of departments, have special needs for professional development.*
- 5.7 *A new grade of 'course assistant' or 'course manager' should be developed.*
- 6.0 *The changes needed require a central initiative.*
- 6.1 *A national body is needed to co-ordinate some aspects of professional development.*
  - a Some professional development is best organized by an independent national body.
  - b A central clearing house is needed for some kinds of professional development.
  - c But the need for systematic evaluation is not an argument for a central body.
- 6.2 *A co-ordinator is needed to service those with special responsibilities for professional development.*
  - a 'Professional developers' also need to develop their skills.
  - b Members of a national body can give personal support for professional development.
  - c A national body is required to pursue research, and to disseminate knowledge on higher education, particularly that which is relevant to professional development.
  - d A national body is required to keep the evaluation of professional development under review.
- 6.3 *A national body is necessary to promote professional development policies.*
  - a There needs to be a national focus for consensus on professional development issues.
  - b Professional development needs national advocates.
  - c A national body is needed to promote national policies for professional development.
  - d Formal qualifications for teaching in higher education should be introduced when they could be acceptable.
- 6.4 *The establishment of a national organization for professional development across all higher education requires an initiative at government level.*
  - a The decision to finance a national organization for professional development requires government initiative.
  - b The Department of Education and Science should establish a working party to consider the form, title, management and finance of a national organization for professional development in higher education.

PROPOSITION 1.0 THE PROFESSIONAL DEVELOPMENT OF TEACHING NEEDS TO BE PLANNED.

With one exception, all the papers submitted to this seminar explicitly assert the need for the planned professional development of teachers in higher education. The reasons for these assertions are twofold. First there is the constant need to improve the quality of all we do. Second there is a recognition that we will have to change what we do in response to changes in higher education.

Just as the development of music means more than improved performances, by the development of teaching I mean more than what is sometimes called 'staff development'. It includes improvements and changes in our knowledge, facilities, research, and so on.

Proposition 1.1 Improvements are needed.

Since the Robbins Report there have probably been more attempts to improve the quality of teaching in higher education than in any comparable period. Never before has the government commissioned reports on university teaching methods (Hale 1963) or audio-visual aids (Brynmor Jones 1965). The Open University has implemented new systems of learning. The CNAA has brought new standards of accreditation. The use of overhead projectors, television, language laboratories, computer assisted learning, photocopiers, and now word processors, widens the repertoire of teaching methods a teacher could possess. The Society for Research into Higher Education is only one of several learned societies established to raise educational standards. Other learned societies (eg the British Psychological Society) have established sub-groups to promote the learning of their subject. The foundation of the Technician Education Council and the Business Education Council shows a concern with the standards of post-secondary teaching outside the education system itself. Amongst the teachers themselves innovations in teaching have been widespread (Nuffield Newsletters 1973-75) and the very fact that the Nuffield Foundation sponsored a group to visit, record and publicize these developments, and continued to offer pump-priming funds to support innovations in teaching, is tantamount to a recognition of the importance of attempts to improve the quality of teaching in higher education. Most significant of all in the context of this chapter, at the time of the Robbins Report virtually no institutions of higher learning in the UK made regular provision for the 'training of new lecturers'; almost no university or polytechnic now makes no provision at all (Matheson 1982)

Yet, in spite of these attempts to improve teaching, developments have been too few and too slow, and concerted plans for its improvement are long overdue. Only a small minority of the teachers in higher education have been involved. We should not ignore the repeated complaints of students about the poor quality of teaching, whether or not we think they are justified. Survey after survey (eg evidence to the Hale Committee 1963, the NUS Report 1969, and the Manchester survey 1979, to mention only three in the past 20 years) seems to suggest that disenchantment is not confined to a vocal minority.

Students are not the only ones to seek improvements. Many of us who teach are aware that we fall short on the very criteria we claim to hold most highly. We value depth of knowledge but we have little knowledge about teaching. We esteem research, but we ourselves do little research into teaching, and we are ignorant of educational research done by others. We may recommend that industrialists monitor their processes of production, but few of us regularly evaluate our own teaching. In many disciplines we exact the highest standards of measurement and judgement from our research students, yet we have the most sublime confidence in our personal impressions of interviewees or examination papers (Dale 1959). We expect to be meticulous in our research procedures, but we may be idiosyncratic in the design of our procedures for student assessment (Elton 1982). While commenting on the finer points of statistical research, we will happily add together raw scores for students on examinations with widely differing means and standard deviations. We may propose radical innovations in government while remaining conservative in academic affairs (Halsey and Trow 1971). We may deplore the abuse of vested interests in business and government while using all means to protect our own on senate. While holding high ideals about objectivity in research, the impartiality of true learning, the detachment of wisdom and the international community of scholars, we are intensely and parochially departmental in our loyalties. While upholding the importance of public scrutiny in the evaluation of research, many of us resist the slightest infringement of absolute privacy in teaching. While recommending discernment and refinement in scholarship, our selection of teaching methods is crude. While many of us see ourselves as innovators in society, the developments in teaching mentioned at the beginning are small compared with changes in schools and the possibilities of educational technology. Most of all, while many of us applaud the benefits of residence in college, the cultural influence of a university, the environment of like-minded people dedicated to learning, and the enthusiastic reponsiveness of students to the excitement of teaching near the frontiers of knowledge, the truth is that our relationships are frequently authoritarian, paternalistic and fearful (see for example Marris 1964, Malleson 1962 and 1967, Wankowski 1973, King 1973, Chandler 1977, Raaheim and Wankowski 1981). All too often students are afraid to seek academic help from us (Wheeler, in press). They dare not tell us, either during a lecture or afterwards, that our lectures are incomprehensible (Sparkes and Black 1982). They are nervous about contributions in tutorials (Bramley 1977). They are anxious about examinations (Still 1963). Research students are afraid to admit ignorance to their supervisors (Katz and Hartnett 1979). They smart under the embarrassment of exposure or criticism in seminars (Mechanic 1978). For many students private study is a time of unvoiced anxiety, uncertain direction and frustrated accomplishment (Malleson 1962). They are taught by those who experienced this agony least and have little memory of it. The content of curricula is not something on which students are consulted or even entitled to venture an opinion. Higher education is about criticism and judgement, but students must accept the curricula laid down without expressing either. There is often an apartheid at teabreak and other times, not only between students and teachers, but between administrators, technicians, porters and any number of other groups. Surely this is not the climate in which our ideals of higher education can thrive? Surely this is not our vision for a 'higher' education of the future? The remedy lies in the development of personal relationships and professional techniques.

Proposition 1.2 Changes are needed.

Above all it is these relationships and the conception of our role that we need to change. To say that we need to be managers of learning is almost a cliché. Yet, as Graham Gibbs has pointed out (1982), we resist changing to this role even when we accept the arguments for doing so. Several strands of the report submitted to the seminar by Black and Sparkes (1982) converge to stress the importance of students understanding how they learn, of students taking responsibility for their learning, of courses directed towards students' development, of staff showing greater understanding of students' feelings, and of staff and students together planning courses to achieve explicit aims.

Underlying the recommendations on assessment, the curriculum and continuing education in the first of these two SRHE Leverhulme volumes on the teaching function (Bligh 1982), is the same plea for a shift in our values: that our teaching should be less expository and more student-centred. For example the chapter on continuing education argues for flexible curricula, 'the diversity of acceptable selection criteria', 'a universal entitlement to continuing education', openness to new teaching methods and the provision of higher education during the evenings and weekends. All these things are sought in the interests of the students, not the staff. The very title of Elton's chapter, 'Assessment for Learning', shows an emphasis not usually associated with examinations. While in some ways the curriculum chapter is very traditional in its restatement of academic values, it is student-, rather than subject-centred in its demand for general courses, wider access to higher education, greater use of projects and the intercalation of practical experience with academic work.

Proposition 1.3 Policies and planning are needed.

Yet the call for student-centred teaching is not new. The arguments for focusing upon students' difficulties in learning, as well as lecturers' difficulties in teaching, are familiar. The need to pay more attention to relationships between teachers and their students is well recognized. So what should we do when we fail to act upon arguments we accept, or fail to respond to needs we recognize? I believe one thing we should not do is 'nothing'. We have seen enough to realize that improvements do not happen of their own accord and the necessary response to changes in higher education in the coming years will not occur by chance. Improvements and changes need planning. Plans need procedures for their implementation. That may seem obvious; but many colleges and institutes of higher education have no well established procedures to improve their teachers' teaching or their students' learning, and it is questionable whether universities have adequate procedures either (cf Matheson 1981). The same conclusion may be drawn from Chapter 1 in this volume, on staffing in higher education: if there are to be new incentives for innovation, career change, refreshment and retraining, policies for their introduction must be planned. If morale is to be maintained when there is 'rationalization of tenure', low staff mobility and little opportunity for promotion, some means of reassurance and some way to cultivate and diversify the skills of staff must be found. If there are to be 'regular reviews of staff performance', there should also be provision to assist improvement. If cross-institutional comparisons of unit costs might encourage undesirable educational practices, a common background of educational principles could help to maintain standards. This series of 'ifs' could be greatly extended, but the general point is clear: if staff are expected to adapt to changes, there should be policies and established procedures to help them do so.

These policies and procedures are for 'staff', and 'professional', development. I don't care what name is used. I am concerned with improvements and changes of the kind I have described. The descriptions are not exhaustive — how could they be? — not all changes can be anticipated. But these improvements and changes will be amongst the aims of people concerned with professional development in the next fifteen years.

The aim of professional development could be defined as 'the improvement, adaptation and advancement of members of a profession in their work'. Such aims are necessarily general. They involve staff who are not teachers and they include activities other than teaching; but this chapter is primarily concerned with 'the teaching function'.

Restriction to 'the teaching function' should not deceive the reader into supposing that the development of teachers and teaching are the only, or necessarily the most important, aims of professional development in higher education. Indeed the solutions to many problems in higher education not closely connected to 'the teaching function' may include programmes of professional development. For example many polytechnic staff were not originally recruited for their research expertise, but are now expected to do research. Many university staff have no experience of industry, but may soon find that they must foster industrial collaboration. Many staff who formerly worked in monotechnic colleges of education may need a very different outlook in institutions that are more broadly based. Other staffs who have had security of tenure may need to acquire a more commercial approach. If the need for flexibility within institutions makes fewer and large departments advantageous, some staff may need to adjust to a new working style. This list could be greatly extended and it is of some regret that this, like other publications on professional development in higher education, will neglect the issues the list raises.

Given aims restricted to changes and improvements in teaching, how can they be achieved?

PROPOSITION 2.0 PLANS TO CHANGE AND IMPROVE TEACHING WILL NEED TO BE BASED UPON METHODS SHOWN TO BE FEASIBLE.

What can be done to achieve these aims? We can only answer this if we know what is feasible. Plans and policies will be useless if they cannot be implemented. Although new methods are to be encouraged, the methods being used to achieve these aims now must be the starting point to judge what is feasible.

I believe it would be generally accepted that the aims of professional development entail the acquisition of knowledge (Proposition 2.1); the development of feelings, personal relationships and powers of inter-personal perception (Proposition 2.2); the improvement of practical skills (Proposition 2.3); and the art of politics and decision making in educational institutions (Proposition 2.4).

Methods that have been used to achieve these aims are listed below. In this section I am not concerned to join the debates about which aims are the most important, which methods are the best, what knowledge and abilities teachers in higher education should possess, or what the content of professional development programmes should be. I quite accept that the aims could be classified in other ways (see Shore 1979 and Harding et al. 1981) and that some professional developers will emphasize some aims more than others. (Phillips (1979) has even suggested that the emphases may be associated with different personality types.) My concern is to say that plans and policies for professional development should not assume that one group of methods should be practised to the exclusion of others. Many approaches could be legitimate and feasible using the methods below.

Proposition 2.1 Acquisition of knowledge is needed.

It may be natural for intellectuals to assume that professional development will result from a knowledge and understanding of 'the principles of teaching' and that academic staff will be able to apply their knowledge to what they do. Accordingly it might be thought that professional development services should have an emphasis upon the presentation of information and research, and the use of audio-visual aids, computer assisted instruction and the latest technology.

Professional development services likely to increase teachers' knowledge include:

1. The production of a newsletter and other publications, the development of a library and the provision of a clearing house for information (eg the Aston *Current Awareness Bulletin,* SRHE and Kingston Polytechnic *Abstracts*, and the newsletters at Birmingham and Leeds.)
2. The provision of short, informal courses, usually on teaching and learning, and sometimes including consideration of local administration. (These are usually for new staff.)
3. Formal courses leading to qualifications (eg the Hatfield Polytechnic, City and Surrey University Course).
4. Study leave and attendance at conferences (see Greenaway and Harding 1978).
5. The conduct of inquiries and research normally into some aspect of the institution, perhaps in comparison with others. In addition, some centres for professional development provide self-evaluation and self-teaching materials with reference to teaching in higher education (eg the distance-teaching materials now being developed at the University of Surrey (Elton 1977 and Elton and Manwaring 1981)).

Although professional development to assist the acquisition of knowledge is impeccably consistent with academic values and is, in the long run, essential to the credibility of professional development services, few people actively engaged in professional development work today would regard it as sufficient on its own. In particular, it does not deal with the personal needs of individuals.

Proposition 2.2 Personal development is needed.

A second approach to professional development emphasizes personal development. Here developers are particularly inclined to assert the individual and voluntary nature of professional development and that courses and other activities should not be prescribed by institutional policies. They are sometimes inclined to be sceptical about the value of research findings that seem to make generalizations without giving sufficient weight to the specific circumstances of a particular social milieu (see, for example, Parlett 1977). They find that the rewards of professional development are to be found in enhanced personal and job satisfactions. They will emphasize experiential learning, self-awareness, inner feelings, the importance of personality, and the general importance of personal circumstances on the performance of both staff and students. They will rightly point out that student drop-out is less associated with intellectual limitations than with personal problems and the socio-emotional problems of adjustment to higher education.

Their professional development services will include:

1 Counselling (eg at Strathclyde; see also Boud and McDonald 1982).
2 Consultation with individuals or groups of staff (eg Hewton 1979).
3 Unstructured discussions (see Sayer 1977).
4 The long term development of groups with a high degree of trust. (see Heron 1982).

Personal development activities are intensely rewarding to some individuals and abhorrent to others. If provided as part of a professional development service they can be offered to few because they are very time consuming. This is not a criticism. On the contrary, proponents of this approach will say that anything else is mere window dressing until the interpersonal problems are tackled that are described by Black and Sparkes (1982). Unfortunately this approach has frequently been misunderstood and it has been criticized for not teaching the practical skills which are complementary to it.

Proposition 2.3 Practical skills are required.

More than in most fields, those in professional development have emphasized the development of practical skills. With a desire to get away from formal courses which appear to have no effect upon professional behaviour, they have typically provided:

1 Microteaching simulations, workshops, games, role-playing and other ways to practise specific skills (see, for example, Brown 1978). Indeed workshops have been the 'in method' of those actively engaged in professional development in higher education in the past ten years (eg Matheson 1978). Sometimes the word has been misused to describe activities that are little more than small group discussions, while originally the method had an emphasis upon simulating participants' working behaviour.
2 Reading, study skills and other practical training for students (eg Main 1980 and Wheeler, in press).

One might also expect that they would favour:
3　Job exchanges and temporary redeployment as a means of widening practical experience in the future (see Civil Service Dept. 1974). There is no doubt that training in practical skills is popular with academic staff who can face the self-scrutiny that, for example, studying video-recordings of one's own teaching requires.

Proposition 2.4　Organizational development is needed.

The fourth group of professional development activities is closely associated with decision making, management studies and organizational development. In Britain as a whole there has always been a tendency for those who wish to bring about educational change to believe that it cannot be done without changing the system as a whole; but in professional development within higher education this tendency has been resisted because it is recognized that professional development can make no progress unless it is in accord with the values of those it seeks to serve (see Proposition 3.1).

Methods to assist with organizational development have included:

1　Country house-party weekends for groups of academics and administrators in pairs (cf Piper and Glatter 1975 and Harding et al. 1981).
2　Working parties to redesign whole curricula rather than tamper with teaching skills in isolation.
3　Exercises for training in management skills (Isaacs 1979 and Jalling 1979).
4　Political activity such as committee work, visiting departments and raising the status of professional development work. It is worth noting in passing that the whole SRHE Leverhulme Study into the Future of Higher Education could be seen as a process of organizational development. It is not concerned to push any particular view, but to raise issues for public debate so as to advance the process of consensus for change.

Conclusion
The activities listed above are being carried out. They are to some extent feasible. To this extent they are a background to the feasibility of professional development plans; but that fact alone tells us nothing about their effectiveness or adequacy. The effectiveness of these methods is constrained by their acceptability (pages 65 ff.), the ease or difficulty of their implementation (pages 67 ff.), and the support for professional development both institutionally (pages 75 ff.) and nationally (pages 85 ff.).

PROPOSITION 3.0 PLANS MUST OBTAIN THE COMMITMENT OF SOCIAL AND WORKING GROUPS.

Proposition 3.1 To be effective, professional development must be in accord with, or close to, the values of the basic social and working groups.

Professional development activities cannot be effective, that is they cannot bring about the desired changes, unless they are acceptable to those of us who are expected to change. This is almost a truism in so far as those expected to change have autonomy. To the extent that they do not, professional development activities will only be accepted in so far as they are tolerated by those who exert power. To a limited extent people tolerate the activities of others with different aims and values; but there comes a point where the limits of tolerance are reached. Hence the limits of professional development are circumscribed by those who exert power.

Those who exert most power are not necessarily those who are most powerful. As individuals vice-chancellors, polytechnic directors and college principals may have the most power, but they may choose not to exert it. Similarly heads of department may exert no strong influence upon whether their staff attend special professional development activities.

In practice the most potent power in higher education institutions lies within the basic social and working groups. These groups are normally academic departments or sub-groups of departments. The source of their power lies in the social and psychological interdependence of group members. There is nothing unusual in that, nor does the statement of this fact imply any approval or disapproval of it. It is true of most groups and there seems no good reason to suppose that as academics we are any different.

Social and working groups have this power firstly because we want to be socially accepted by our group and secondly because the group influences the development of our ideas. As in other groups our dominant values are more often social than intellectual. They are to do with acceptance and esteem, friendship and reputation. Of these, acceptance and friendship are the more important because they are the more immediate. The rewards of esteem and reputation are more long-term. In so far as intellectual esteem and reputation are both social values, they are public to the academic groups in which we move, and we strive to maximize our performance on those criteria which are public enough for the groups to judge. Of course, these include academic criteria such as publications, but they also include social criteria such as being friendly, relaxed, lively and good humoured.

When someone is socially accepted as a 'good chap', or as 'good colleague', or a 'friend' his ideas are perceived as more acceptable. In particular the acceptability of professional development will be influenced by the social acceptability of its proponents. Whatever changes in teaching might be proposed, the proposals will achieve nothing without the consent of the teachers who must implement them. In so far as improvements and changes in teaching depend upon the teachers' consent, they depend upon the teachers' beliefs, ideas and attitudes, which are inevitably strongly influenced by the social and working groups to which the teachers belong. Admittedly many academics are intellectually very independent, but it is probably also true that we spend more time than most groups influencing each other by sharing and testing ideas. Paradoxically, although in many ways independence is strongly encouraged, we know that we are dependent upon the approval of our peers.

I have described these groups as 'social' and 'working'. They are social in that their members meet, talk and laugh together. Interaction between their members is close and repeated. There is mutual support and dependence upon approval. The groups have their own vested interests, and their group cohesion is strengthened when these interests are threatened by other groups. Members share some property in common of which 'their' students (over whom they have sanctions, whose attendance they can command, whom they may select and whom they can assess) are the most important. Group members may have their own building, or part of one. They have their own territory in the Senior Common Room and, however polite their conversation, their body language makes invaders unwelcome, uncomfortable and conscious of the intrusion. Their conversation is about their immediate and everyday concerns to which others are not expected to contribute and probably can't. They frequently play a part in selecting other group members. In so far as they teach the same students, teach closely related parts of the same subject, read a strongly overlapping literature, use the same accommodation, go to conferences where they meet others from the same academic sub-culture, talk the same language and share the same patterns of thinking, they have a common experience both within and outside their institution that is not shared by others within it.

These groups are sub-cultures of academe. I use anthropologists' language, partly to induce some detachment in readers from higher education; but also to show that 'professional developers' could all too easily be cast in the role of colonialists claiming to come from a superior culture.

No policies for professional development, or indeed for anything else, can afford to ignore the effective power of these groups. No recommendations that ignore them will be effective in the long run.

Once the power and influence of the basic social and working groups is clear, it will be apparent that, to be effective, professional development work must obtain consensual support within these groups.

Proposition 3.2 Basic social and working groups are, and will be, the main instruments of professional development.

(i) Because of the influence of the social and working groups, whatever professional development work formally takes place elsewhere, it is in these groups that most professional development takes place. In professional development it is personal relationships that are influential. The courses, meetings, workshops and similar activities that I, and other professional developers, organize may have an influence greater than the proportion of an academic's time spent at them (McMillan 1975); but we should have no illusions that their effects are drowned into insignificance by all the time an academic spends actually doing his job (rather than talking about it) and by the influence of his closer colleagues.

Hence the social and working groups are the main instruments of professional development. The surveys by CCTUT and others on what formal courses for academic staff are being provided by institutions are not irrelevant, but, like much professional development work itself, they fail to get behind the surface of formal activity. (This is not a criticism. What other information could be sought? One cannot survey personal relationships. It merely draws attention to the practical limitations of policies and 'legislation'.)

(ii) The second point is to recognize that the place of the social and working groups as the main instruments of professional development is unlikely to change. The natures of personal relationships and group dynamics are not going to change at the request of a committee deciding plans for professional development.

(iii) I hope the conclusion is obvious. Policies for professional development must recognize the power of the basic groups and plan to use it. To do so they must obtain the support, consensus and active commitment of these groups. But, as we shall see in the next section, support, consensus and commitment will be very difficult to obtain.

PROPOSITION 4.0 THE DIFFICULTIES IN IMPLEMENTING PROFESSIONAL DEVELOPMENT PLANS NEED TO BE RECOGNIZED AT A SENIOR LEVEL.

Proposition 4.1 Basic social and working groups are, by their nature, resistant to change.

There are obvious exceptions to this generalization. It is not difficult to think of isolated innovative groups working enthusiastically designing new courses or using new methods; but as a proportion of all the thousands of staff employed, they are few. Nor is it difficult to think of examples, particularly in the polytechnics, when circumstances outside a group have demanded important and lasting changes in methods of assessment or the teamwork of staff; but examples of similar importance initiated within a group are less common. Again, although we can all think of recent additions to our syllabus, it is more difficult to think of recent deletions; and this may have something to do with an unwillingness to change what we are doing.

I do not mean to imply that, as teachers in higher education, we are unconcerned or idle in matters of teaching. Conscientiousness is very evident, but most groups are unwilling, and possibly unable, to reconsider, for example, the teacher-centred style of teaching which predominates. Such a change requires too big a shift in attitudes and most basic groups do not have the knowledge and experience to deal with all the problems that might arise from a radical change in teaching style. Still less do I want to commit the missionary's fallacy of supposing that, 'If only the multitude of teachers would abandon their present ineffective rituals and accept a new way of life preached by professional developers, then all would be well'.

Nonetheless in the practice of teaching in higher education academics have been unresponsive to the need for change; the areas needing improvement listed in Proposition 1.1 are not new. Student disenchantment with university teaching did not start with the discontent of 1968 or at Berkeley in 1964. Einstein, Darwin and Dr Johnson are only three of many whose complaints have for a long time gone unheeded.

Since academic staff are, in many matters outside their institution, considerably more radical than a typical member of the population (Halsey and Trow 1971), how is it that they should appear conservative in their own affairs? One answer is that change, particularly change demanded by others, is seen as a threat to the autonomy of the group. Demands for changes in teaching are perceived as a threat to one's personal image (see Proposition 4.2).

Another answer is that it is difficult to obtain the consensus of a whole group because, when one change is made, it is soon found that others are necessary and very soon the limits of tolerance of some group members are reached. Hence changes can produce an instability which is only removed by a return to the status quo. The history of education is full of revolutionary ideas that never 'catch on' (possibly for good reason: eg programmed learning or the Dalton Plan). The forces for conservatism in higher education seem strong.

The very internal forces that bind a group as a group are those that establish the norms of the group and thereby establish implicit rules and a group consensus that innovators must question and then break. The success of developments in teaching is always uncertain. The rewards are likely to be few. Still less do they seem likely to justify the risks and effort, unless the risks of not changing seem greater.

Of course resistance can be overcome by a stronger force. Such a prospect raises the question of when, if at all, professional development should be 'encouraged' by anything stronger than the provision of opportunities. Proponents of a strong line might point to developments in courses over the past twenty years. Don't the achievements of polytechnics in part reflect their response to the pressures of validation processes? Would the former colleges of education be diversifying their courses as they are now if they were not subject to considerable pressures? On the other hand little pressure to diversify courses was applied to the universities at the time of the 'Robbins expansion' (although Robbins said that the provision of broader courses was 'an essential condition' attached to his principle). Admittedly some new universities responded to the opportunity (eg Sussex), but it is probably fair to say that broader courses were not a major element of expansion in existing universities. It is too early to say whether the present cuts will cause universities to provide new kinds of courses (eg short and part-time courses), but if they do, it will be tempting to interpret these events as showing that carrots produce fewer developments than sticks.

The implications of the 'strong line' argument could be serious if accepted by people outside higher education. One answer in the case of professional development is to show that the provision of opportunities is equally effective.

Proposition 4.2 Professional development is easily perceived as a threat to an individual's self-esteem.

A major difficulty in the development of teaching lies in the feelings of academic staff on this subject. Those working to improve teaching in higher education are constantly aware that their work arouses anxiety and hostility from colleagues who, on other matters, can be relied upon for dispassionate judgement. This makes the advancement of policies in a democratic institution extremely hazardous.

Hostility may appear without any previous contact having been made. In one university a newly appointed member of staff responsible for professional development wished to introduce himself to heads of department. He was given an appointment at 8.30 in the morning by one professor who shouted at him that he was unwelcome in the department, that he, the professor, had opposed the creation of the new post and that he disapproved of all professional development work on principle. Recently, in a well-known college, attempts to involve departmental advisors in helping new members of staff were thwarted by heads of departments imposing meetings, teaching and administration at the time they were supposed to have been freed to attend a course. When asked to send the policy recommendations for this publication one correspondent sent four closely-typed pages of confidential remarks expressing a series of frustrations in his work resulting from the attitude of senior academic staff. In another university the member of staff responsible for staff development has more than once been subjected to physical assault.

I give these examples, and many others could be given, to show that the weight of feeling is often far greater than its immediate source would seem to justify. To anyone stressing the importance of personal relationships in higher education they are hard to ignore! It seems difficult to escape the conclusion that quite strong emotional forces are involved.

These feelings need to be understood, not condemned. What is the source of this emotion or energy? Has it been pent up for some time, and if so, what are the features of the college or university climate that repress it? Why should people engaged in professional development be recipients of such aggression? After all, their role is to help their colleagues. Is it to do with the way their work, role or status is perceived; or do they, by some incompetence, invite such abuse?

There could be many answers to these questions and they need to be researched. In the absence of firm evidence, any answer must be speculation. However after discussion with colleagues in universities and polytechnics I suspect three factors about the feelings of academic staff need a sympathetic understanding. Each is concerned with the self-esteem of academic staff.

One is that professional developers create an image that is threatening. For example they are often expected to provide short courses for staff at which, if the courses are to satisfy personal needs, professional developers must make personal judgements about their colleagues. Even when personal judgements are not made participants may think that they are. The very appointment of professional developers could be interpreted as a criticism of normal teaching standards. Perhaps the fullness of time and the 'training' of professional developers will produce ways to modify these perceptions.

Another factor is that professional development involves gaining knowledge about oneself and about one's personal relationships in particular. Knowledge about oneself can be disturbing, particularly for older staff. When first appointed a new teacher is dependent upon the appointing committee and the power of the head of department. His self-esteem is not threatened by the suggestion that he is inexperienced at teaching, because he obviously is; but when autonomy is being sought, when the pretence that all is well in the classroom has been presented to the basic social group over the coffee cups, when he begins to neglect his teaching in favour of those activities that are better rewarded, when he realizes that his teaching difficulties lie in his failure to establish personal relationships with his students, and when he (incorrectly) believes that he lacks sufficient knowledge to teach what is required, it is difficult to confess inadequacy. Such confessions require an inner security to face oneself which is not to be found in those who most need help.

Thirdly, many teachers don't want to engage in activities in which they think they will be cast in a learner's role. Their self-esteem within the institution depends upon their seeing themselves as having some authority, both in their subject and in their teaching. Any teacher who has this conception of his role lives continually in the fear that his authority, status, expertise and power will be challenged (see for example Cowan 1979). (True, many academics say that they want students to question what they say and to argue against it; but they often only want this if they can win the argument in the end.) A consequence is that if this authoritarian conception of the teaching relationship is accepted, to attend a course, or even a single meeting, on teaching will be misconceived as acknowledging the presence of the authority, status and expertise of another person in matters of teaching. But when they teach this is an image they take upon themselves. When they teach they assume they know what is good for their students. They decide the course. They decide how it is to be taught and in what order. They set the standards. From the assumption of authority they are didactic and assume control. To accept the authority of another on matters of teaching is to deprecate their own. It threatens their self-image at precisely the place where they need it to be bolstered daily. Furthermore, authoritarian teachers may feel that to admit they have learned something is to admit a former inadequacy. It is to admit that for years their teaching was not as good as it might have been. The longer a teacher's experience, the more his self-image requires him to say that he has learned nothing.

The previous paragraph may seem like a criticism and in one sense it is; but there is no blame involved. On the contrary we have seen enough of the power of the basic groups to realize that when a new teacher enters a department, there is little or no way he can change the pattern of relationships that may have existed for decades. Particularly in the university sector, the desire for esteem perpetuates a system of social divisions which, in my experience, is only exceeded in the Health Service. Our paternalistic assumptions about the nature of higher education represent students as members of a lower social order who would humiliate the aristocracy if they offered any kind of help. Few staff ask students to help them with their teaching. Yet surely students, if approached in the right way, could make important contributions. The 'us and them' relationship is, in my view, antithetical to the values of higher education. In the long run we have a common purpose in the pursuit of learning.

All this is made worse by an under-recognized fact. In teaching we fail much of the time. Teaching is an art. As for a violinist struggling to do better next time, there are no absolute rules. There are continual compromises. Of course, we try hard and we have our successes, but in the long run, not only is perfection impossible, but our failures seem to be beyond our control. We depend upon our students for success.

Compared with the population as a whole most academics are relatively unaccustomed to failure. Within the educational system of which they are now a member, they have usually been very successful. When they have failed they have worked hard to overcome their disappointments. But teaching ultimately brings frustration because continual failure is normal and beyond our control. It is well known that frustration often generates aggression. Ultimately the only way to deal with it is to ignore the source of frustration. Thus below a surface of indifference to teaching there often lies a passionate unease. An academic can hold his head up high providing the privacy of his teaching is maintained, and provided his unease is not taken out and paraded for all to see. Reputation and acceptance are crucial within academic groups.

Proposition 4.3 'Professional developers' themselves need professional development.

Another difficulty in implementing plans for professional development is the inexperience of the staff required to do it. Professional developers, too, need professional development.

It is not easy for heads of departments to adopt the professional developer's role. Heads of departments who advise on teaching are soon conscious of an ambiguous relationship with their staff; they may be sensitive to students' comments about their own teaching; and they may believe that their position as head of department was earned more through their research than their teaching. Consequently, some heads of departments are glad to leave professional development to 'professional developers' outside their department.

Yet being outside the social and working groups gives these professional developers considerable difficulties, particularly in so far as they adopt the approach I have called *personal development* (Proposition 2.2). There is a need for professional developers to establish the trust of their colleagues, to overcome the threats to self-esteem and to appreciate the personal abilities and limitations of individual members of staff in the context of each particular working group. This takes time. The development of personal relationships cannot be hurried. How much time does the developer have? In an institution with 460 academic staff, they would each have one hour per year of the professional developer's time if he devoted 10 hours per week for 46 weeks to individual contact, or an equivalent 'teaching' load of 15 hours per week for 30 weeks. Obviously one hour per year will achieve little or nothing. The alternative is to work with only a fraction of the staff or to work with groups rather than individuals. I give these figures to show the difficulty, if not the impossibility, of a professional developer alone making much institutional impact (see Black and Sparkes 1982). He, too, needs professional development to manage his personal relationships and to optimize his use of time.

For those who see professional development as *organizational development* (Proposition 2.4) or a 'political activity' within an institution, power and judgement are important. Yet few professional developers occupy positions of power and most have no prospect of doing so. Ironically, there is no career structure for professional developers. Furthermore, if professional developers are constantly subjected to the emotional pressures described in the last section, it is difficult to avoid errors of judgement. Errors in professional development affect relationships. Compared with errors of judgement in teaching, the penalties can be long lasting — students leave after three years; staff do not. Hence, again, the conscious development of developers seems vital.

If a more didactic approach to developing *practical skills* (Proposition 2.3) by short courses or workshops is adopted, developers must quickly learn a new range of teaching techniques. They need to earn their credibility and sell their programme on the first morning of a course, because academics are quick to pass judgements. Short courses must run without a hitch because there is no time to correct errors or to compensate for organizational breakdowns. While flexibility is essential, courses require planning at a high level of detail because they often take place in vacations when normal services are not available. Bearing in mind the sensitivity of their subject matter, not only do professional developers have to develop a supportive group climate in a way that most academics never have to do, but they have to do it in a few hours rather than over a period of several weeks. They cannot compel attendance; they have no sanctions; they offer no rewards or certificates; so every period of teaching must be attractive and immediately relevant. Consequently, a thorough grounding in the basics of their subjects is often unsaleable.

There are many other characteristics that make this kind of teaching exceptionally demanding. Developers must demonstrate a wide range of teaching skills all to a high level of competence. A large proportion of participants are intellectually their equal or superiors. Their participants have very varied perspectives and attach great weight to very different features of a course all of which must therefore be at a high standard. Those only used to academic courses are unsettled by teaching for inter-personal perception. It is difficult to be relevant for all participants all the time. Higher education is a field with many disciplines and developers need some combination of breadth and depth if they are to remain academically credible. Their teaching must be innovative, and their reputation is at stake if they fail in a way that is not true for most teachers in higher education.

All in all the differences in sheer professional technique between those of the professional developer and undergraduate teachers are just as great as the differences between undergraduate teaching and school teaching. They reinforce the need for conscious professional development for people with special responsibility for the professional development of others. People with this responsibility include not only those explicitly appointed with this brief, but also heads of departments and members of the professional development committee. This may seem like special pleading. It is — and with good reason. There is virtually no context in which professional developers can make these plans for themselves without personal embarrassment.

Although professional development by the *acquisition of knowledge* is a less stormy path, it has two major difficulties. The first is that a professional developer needs a very wide academic background if he is to have a mature understanding of the limitations of educational research in the fields of psychology, philosophy, sociology, economics and so on.

The second is that there is an inadequate basis of knowledge for professional development.

Proposition 4.4 There is an inadequate basis of knowledge for professional development.

Any proposal for the future of professional development must include recommendations to increase our knowledge of what is to be changed by that development. Ultimately the justification of a professional development programme must be in research. Developers need to know a lot more about what is feasible. We know little about how staff change, if they do, during their careers. Much of higher education is shrouded in confidentiality and the sensitivity of professional issues makes large samples, and hence reasonable generalizations, extremely difficult to obtain. Yet the very sensitivity of the subject makes justification all the more necessary.

No doubt academics are always complaining that more research needs to be done in the disciplines in which they work, but there are reasons why the study of higher education itself is a particularly needy case. A recent paper published by the Society for Research into Higher Education (1982) draws attention to a vicious circle suppressing significant development of research into higher education. Lack of finance for research into higher education leads to inadequate provision of courses in this field, few training opportunities, few teachers to develop research techniques, a lack of organized centres for research, poor development of the field and consequently poor opportunities for its participants to obtain finance to develop it.

It is not only research but scholarship that is needed. We need to gather our knowledge about higher education and attempt re-interpretations of it. Furthermore, the fact that higher education is divided into two or three sectors means that comprehensive surveys are few, that the students differ, and that cost comparisons are difficult.

However, the fact that research into higher education is difficult does not mean that it is impossible. It needs a financial stimulus and a firm organization outside institutions of higher education themselves. SRHE is not strong enough at present. The need for such an organization is not a sufficient reason to establish a higher education development council, but it there were other compelling reasons, research would naturally be part of its function.

Any proposals for the future of professional development must include recommendations to increase our knowledge of what is to be changed by that development.

Proposition 4.5 The development of teaching will be difficult while incentives seem to favour the development of research.

Whatever protestations are made to the contrary, academics see the shortest path to promotion as through research and publications rather than through teaching, administration and public service. Indeed, in universities, readerships and personal chairs exist for prowess in research and there is no comparable status for good teaching. Similarly, with a few exceptions, there is no generally accepted qualification for teaching in higher education, while degrees may be obtained for research. Professional developers may proclaim the importance of teaching but when there is a conflict of attitudes between those presented in a course for new staff and those of a departmental group, new staff can quickly see which is the most politic to adopt.

The perceptions by academic staff can only be changed by institutional policies to reward teaching being explicitly stated and evidently, if not openly, implemented.

Conclusion
The difficulties associated with professional development are formidable. They cannot be overcome without institutional policies and help from outside organizations. We will consider institutional policies on pages 75—85 and outside help on pages 85 ff.

PROPOSITION 5.0 THERE IS A NEED TO INSTITUTIONALIZE PROFESSIONAL DEVELOPMENT.

Proposition 5.1 There should be institutional policies for professional development.

Nothing said in this section is intended to detract from the importance of professional development within the basic social and working groups. Nonetheless, there are at least three reasons why institutions, as distinct from departments, should have policies for professional development.

First, there are so many aspects of professional development that considerable responsibility for it lies outside the basic social and working groups. For example, consider who takes decisions in connection with promotions, sabbatical leave, the allocation of conference funds, the planning of curricula, the selection of students, opportunities to serve on committees, the organization and techniques of assessment, the evaluation of courses, the need to implement changes recommended by evaluations, liaison with professional bodies, the changing needs of employers, the need to increase staff mobility, changes in academic disciplines, the acquisition and use of external funding and so on. All these things — and the list could easily be extended — affect the professional opportunities and development of individuals. This is not to support centralization or institutional control; but, if institutional management affects opportunities, professional development needs to be monitored regularly. This point will become important if opportunities in higher education become fewer.

Secondly, it is unlikely that all departmental groups will contain sufficient wisdom or experience to foster professional development successfully. Although the use of departmental colleagues has its attractions and forms part of the agreement between the University Authorities Panel and the Association of University Teachers on the probation of new staff (1972), we have seen that it also introduces ambiguous relationships within the basic social and working groups, which ultimately do not lead to harmony unless the senior colleague has very considerable personal skill. Similarly we have seen that the difficulties in implementing professional development plans need to be recognized at a senior level in a polytechnic or university. Professional developers sometimes need advice and support.

Thirdly, and most obviously, some changes in what individuals do will need to be co-ordinated at an institutional level. For example if a polytechnic increases the number of its part-time students, it may need to develop amongst its staff a consultative style in teaching those students. Furthermore, whilst not asserting that everyone needs the same kind of professional development, there are benefits from co-operation across departmental groups.

Proposition 5.2 To pursue professional development policies, institutions should make arrangements consonant with local circumstances.

For many of the people consulted in the preparation of this paper, how professional development should be institutionalized is the crucial question. It is to be expected that the ideal arrangements will vary greatly with the institution. The distinctive patterns of power amongst departments, the peculiar sensitivity of staff and particular institutional circumstances make a diversity of arrangements prudent. Yet I suspect that the contraction of higher education, the need for new methods of teaching and learning, the need to develop new curricula, the need to expand continuing education, the problems of staff immobility, the power of the basic social and working groups, and the difficulties of professional development work will all be sufficiently common across universities, polytechnics and institutes of higher education for the policies and means for professional development to become more homogeneous than the current diversity of, and within, institutions may lead one to expect.

Rutherford (1982) has classified existing institutional arrangements for professional development into four models. In what follows I shall rely heavily on his forthcoming paper and shall quote liberally from it.

Some institutions delegate their responsibility for professional development of teaching to an *independent unit*, frequently consisting of a single person or possibly a small group of staff headed by an academic who, although he reports to an appropriate committee of the institution, has fairly wide terms of reference. The unit is regarded in much the same way as a conventional academic department and its activities are not closely monitored except in times of crisis. 'It is unlikely that the unit will find itself in a powerful political position within its institution and herein lies its main weakness.' 'The success of a unit is heavily dependent upon the academic and political skills of its leader. This is especially true when the unit consists of a single person who, if he is perceived as successful in all or even most quarters of the university, is quite a remarkable person.' The most supportive members of staff are, of course, those who use the unit's services, but these people are unlikely to form a recognized body of support. Consequently members of such units always feel vulnerable to the changing political pressures within an institution. They are too often perceived by those who do not use their services as consuming resources rather than providing or conserving them. Because their benefits to the institution are often intangible, they are frequently dependent for their survival on the vocal support of senior staff at the centres of political influence and power within the institution and of the staff whom they chiefly serve. Without a specialist unit and specialist staff, research-based activities would be difficult to provide and sorely needed research into higher education would develop even more slowly than at present.

In the second approach the institution delegates its responsibilities to a *committee* composed of 'keen teachers' and representatives of various interest groups. The institution has no full or part-time person responsible for professional development. Consequently, although this approach is inexpensive, it relies upon the enthusiasm of committee members who must do this work in addition to their normal duties. The committee differs from many others in that its members not only have a deliberative function, but they themselves carry out their agreed policies, and the process repeats itself year after year. However, while members may enjoy, and gain a great deal from their discussions and participation, their membership is temporary and their commitment takes its toll. The impetus of such activites is difficult to maintain. Furthermore, there is only one such group in the institution at any time, while most institutions probably have several needs which ought to be satisfied at the same time. Provision is conceived in terms of the needs of newly-appointed staff and occasional meetings with interested colleagues throughout the year. While the approach permits the institution to say that it is making some provision and to name persons responsible, its services can come nowhere near to satisfying the needs outlined in the first section of this chapter.

In the third approach the institution delegates its responsibilities to a specially appointed member of staff but also establishes a committee to work closely with him. Hence there is a *semi-independent unit*. The professional developer 'initiates proposals and prepares papers which the committee in turn considers, modifies (if necessary) and approves.' The committee sees its primary role as one of advice and support while the institution regards the committee as bearing ultimate responsibility. The approach appears to combine the advantages of the previous two. The professional developer can provide initiative, time and permanence, while the committee can give political wisdom and credibility. Much depends upon harmony between the chairman of the committee, who is probably a senior academic, and the full-time professional developer. However, the weakness of the approach is that rank and file members of the committee tend to 'rubber stamp' their proposals, feel less responsible, and are relatively passive.

The fourth approach, *the working group*, is regarded with increasing favour amongst professional developers (see Hewton 1979; Conrad 1979). It uses the power of the social and working groups. Members of a committee agree broad policies which are then carried out by small working groups with the support and participation of persons with a full or part-time responsibility for professional development. Typically the groups work on some innovation or curriculum development. A given group has a specific task, the criteria of its accomplishment are clear and there is usually loyalty and commitment to other group members to achieve it. Hence there are gains not only in the achievement, but in personal satisfaction and relationships. The groups are temporary, but come together because of an identified need on which there is consensus. In short the group works within the values, consent and interests of its members, and, because of this fact, many of the difficulties experienced in other forms of professional development are removed. Such activities do not have to be initiated by the professional development committee; they may be requested directly to the professional developer by faculty boards, departments or other groups, in which case the professional developer simply reports his acceptance of the brief to his committee later.

Proposition 5.3 Policies for professional development need to combine institutional authorization at the highest level with a personal sensitivity in their implementation.

'The highest level' probably means a major planning committee of the institution. No doubt this will vary with the institution. (In the Federal Republic of Germany the direct involvement of the university president is more common.) What follows is not intended to be prescriptive. There is a need to recognize and nurture the unique and individual ways in which institutions have approached professional development. The important point is that this is no longer a responsibility that institutions in higher education can afford to neglect at a senior level. The abilities of staff are their chief resources. Particularly at the present time, the way in which these abilities are to be developed could be a major element of institutional policy.

Perhaps a professional development committee should be a subcommittee of a major committee. Its brief might be:

a   To receive professional development plans regularly from heads of departments, others responsible and the individuals directly concerned.
b   To be able to receive requests and appeals from individuals with reference to their own professional development.
c   To recommend, in consultation with individuals, heads of department and possibly the unions, methods for achieving these plans in the light of institutional policies.
d   To oversee and recommend their co-ordination as appropriate.
e   To assist and support persons responsible for professional development, including heads of department and those holding appointments with special responsibilities in this field.
f   To allocate resources for professional development.
g   To initiate, to develop and to evaluate professional development activities.

Respect for the individual is an important principle. Amongst professional developers consulted during the preparation of this chapter there was wide agreement that the jobs listed for a committee as above need to be done. There was less agreement on who should do them. This may be because of the need to reconcile the consent of the individual with the need for co-ordination and prestige at a high level within the institution.

It will be noticed that the role of the professional development committee allows for individuals to plan their own development, thereby creating an opportunity to harmonize the aims of the individual and of the institution.

It places an obligation upon the institution to consider an individual's needs and wishes. It has an extremely difficult task here because it must distinguish expressed and perceived needs from 'real' ones. The philosophical issues raised by this distinction cannot be discussed here; it is sufficient that the reader recognizes that the submission of needs to a committee is open to abuse, but that some kind of submission is necessary if the institution has the power to sanction or withhold resources.

The individual, his group and the institution must work out methods together. Thus responsibility for aims, resources and methods should be distinguished. Much of this could be expedited if a professional development profile for each member of staff were compiled by the individual concerned, by his professional advisers and head of department, and received annually by the professional development committee. This process may seem like manipulative management or unnecessary bureaucracy, but it has usually been appreciated on all sides where it has been tried.

Proposition 5.4 Institutional policies for professional development should include regular reviews of the aims and development of staff.

This proposition may seem to be obvious common sense. Yet although regular staff reviews are common practice in polytechnics they are rarer elsewhere. Insitutions are changing all the time. The changes that are possible in an institution depend upon its resources. How could it plan for change without an inventory of its resources? The major resource of higher education is its staff. There is no point in trying to change or improve staff performance if we don't know what that performance is like in the first place.

Secondly, it is part of staff development that institutions should regularly review the opportunities they can offer their staff. If it is part of the ethos of an educational institution that it cares about the future careers of its students, surely it should have a similar attitude towards the careers of its staff? If there are going to be fewer opportunities for staff in the future there is a risk of growing frustration and discontent. The provision of opportunities cannot be left to laisser faire policies. The frustration caused by immobility of staff can, to some extent, be offset by developing new roles for them. Indeed, job rotation within departments has this effect even though it may not result in the development of the institution. Furthermore, to broaden the experience of individuals increases their mobility by increasing their value to other employers.

A regular review of staff not only facilitates institutional change; it fosters individual improvement. The well known Hawthorne effect seemed to show (admittedly in a very different type of work) that the level of performance is better maintained when the management appears to pay attention to the needs of its staff. Regular reviews can also be a way of showing respect for staff by acknowledging their potential in areas other than those in which they are at present engaged.

Proposition 5.5 There should be systematic and formal procedures for the evaluation of teaching.

A major problem facing institutions in the context of this chapter is how to provide incentives and quality control for teaching. The traditional objection to the formal assessment of teaching is that it cannot be assessed, or, a contradictory statement, that it is assessed and we all know who the good teachers are so that formal evaluation is unnecessary.

The first objection is simply false. Student teachers have long been assessed for practical teaching; and while it may be claimed that teaching in higher education is different from school teaching, it is not so different that it cannot be assessed at all.

The second objection relies on hearsay evidence. Teaching is an academic activity and the evaluation of teaching is therefore concerned with maintaining and raising academic standards. The evaluation of teaching is a process of inquiry. It may not be research in the sense of cutting back the frontiers of knowledge, but to rely on hearsay evidence of who the good teachers are, or to adopt canons of inquiry of a lower standard than the best possible, is hardly to strive for the excellence in which academics take pride. I quite accept that 'the best possible' may, with present knowledge, not be as good as we might wish; but that is no reason why we should not strive for excellence in teaching as well as research.

The objection may then be raised that research is much easier and fairer to assess through publications and reputation amongst colleagues, than through teaching. The point is rarely made that the assessment of research is far from satisfactory and suffers from many of the same difficulties as the evaluation of teaching. Indeed there is a growing literature on the evaluation of teaching. But although there has long been a theoretical literature on principles of research, there is very little on its evaluation. The evaluation of research is usually highly impressionistic. Just as teaching styles cannot easily be compared, there are problems of non-comparability in the evaluation of research.

There are, of course, well known methods for the assessment of doctoral research. The candidate prepares documents and other evidence of what he has done. This will include his own evaluation of it and his recommendations for improvements and later work. It is open to his assessors to question him on his evidence including his choice of criteria, to recommend other approaches and to offer criticism and advice.

Much the same procedures can be adopted in the evaluation of teaching. Two years ago I was invited by a polytechnic to select three teachers for promotion to the grade of principal lecturer on the basis of their teaching and this is broadly the method we used. Members of staff were invited to submit any materials or other evidence they chose which might contribute to this evaluation. The materials included course plans submitted to the Council for National Academic Awards, hand-outs, audio-visual aids, publications, copies of testimonials they had written for others or others had written for them, evidence from student evaluation questionnaires and absolutely any other material they wished. They were given up to an hour (too short) of my time during which they could invite me to observe their teaching, to meet their students or to spend in any other way they chose. They were entitled to invite advocates to speak either with me, or with the directorate, either in the candidate's presence or alone. With their submission they were invited to state the criteria on which they thought their teaching should be assessed. In this way there was respect for a candidate's specific circumstances and the application of uniform criteria was avoided. Finally there were formal interviews with the directorate which contained some identical questions for comparability.

It should be noticed that on this method of evaluation a member of staff's teaching is not assessed by his head of department or those appointed with special responsibility for professional development work; indeed these people are likely to be his advocates and to write testimonials on his behalf. This method of evaluation does not establish ambiguous and fearful relationships either within the basic social and working group or with professional development staff. It also permits the external assessor to be constructive, emphasizing merits and talents which the individual could develop.

It was intended to be an all-embracing method. Certainly it could entail many more specific techniques. Whether the evaluation of teaching is to assess past performance or inform teachers for the future, most of the observations evaluators make can be subsumed under four broad questions: What were the results of the teaching? What did people think of it? Describe exactly what happened, and What was necessary for the teaching to take place? Answers to the first question can sometimes be obtained from the results of examinations and other tests, longitudinal studies of large samples of students, inspection of course work, and experiments. The second question prompts the use of opinionnaires and interviews. Descriptions of what happens on a course can be obtained using diaries, case studies, workload analyses, critical incident techniques, participant observation methods, library records, audio and video recordings, and all kinds of documentary analyses. The last question focuses on the use of resources and partial answers can be obtained using inventories, simulation techniques, modelling and accountancy.

All methods of assessment have their limitations and those mentioned above are not exceptions; but it is simply not true to say that teaching cannot be assessed and that research can. What is true is that most of us have had little practice or training in the evaluation of teaching or in cultivating ways to improve it. Furthermore few of those responsible for evaluating the teaching of their colleagues have read much of the literature on these subjects. The failure to evaluate teaching, and with it the failure to reward those who teach well, is the result of ignorance, not impossibility. This is one area where senior staff are in need of professional development and it is to this we shall now turn.

Proposition 5.6 Senior staff, including heads of departments, have special needs for professional development.

To some senior staff this proposition will be seen as a criticism, if not an insult. It is neither. It is intended to be neutral. It could be seen as a compliment. The belief that this proposition implies a criticism comes from an inappropriate attitude towards learning. It is an attitude that confuses a belief that it is possible to do one's job better with a belief that one is inadequate. Learning is not necessarily remedial and associated with inadequacy and low esteem.

We need to encourage a new attitude to professional development. It is an investment. Those most worthy of professional development are those in whom it is worthy to invest, whose work is important and influential, who are most able to adapt, who are most likely to encourage development in others, and who have the most to contribute. This description should characterize heads of departments and staff rising to positions of seniority.

A more obvious reason for the special needs of heads of departments lies in the fact that promotion to head of department brings new duties requiring new knowledge and new skills. In particular heads of departments need skills in the management of their colleagues. It is they who have the greatest influence upon the social and working groups and commonly within institutions as a whole. They need an understanding of how they are perceived by students and colleagues. Those heads of department promoted primarily on the basis of their research could be those who would benefit most from learning about teaching and administration. Heads of departments have special responsibilities for curriculum planning, the evaluation of teaching, maintaining its standards, the management of examinations and the appointment of staff.

However the fact that an institution recognizes the need to help its senior staff does not mean that it should, itself, provide that help directly. There are good reasons to think that formal professional development activities are better provided in the company of people from institutions other than one's own. Much of the development is personal development of the kind described under Proposition 2.2. It does not necessarily involve personal exposure, as in T-Group management education, but a head of department will want to talk through his own departmental problems in confidence. For dispassionate consideration, the case studies he presents will need to be anonymous to others. Some of his work is 'political' and in competition with other heads of department; it is difficult to see how formal professional development for this work could avoid serious side effects and ambiguous relationships if it were provided by members of an institution to their own colleagues. Prophets from another institution are usually more acceptable and when they are not their 'advice' can be ignored with academic freedom and no local embarrassment. Furthermore, many issues in the professional development of senior staff are discipline-related so that inter-institutional collaboration is particularly appropriate.

If it is accepted that senior staff have needs for professional development that are different from those of their junior colleagues and that at least some of these needs cannot satisfactorily be provided by their own institution, the institution will need a policy to support the external provision of professional development for senior staff.

Proposition 5.7 A new grade of 'course assistant' or 'course manager' should be developed.

Academic staff time could be saved if routine and administrative tasks were performed by someone trained to do them. Most academics are not appointed because of their expertise in producing teaching materials, liaising with industry, keeping course records or monitoring student performance.

What is required for each course team — which may be the same as the social and working group — is a 'course assistant' or 'course manager'. During the preparation of a course the course manager will plan the lead times of preparation, convene meetings of the team, prepare its 'agendas', brief its members, and prepare drafts of course material as required at each stage. During the course itself the course manager will, in co-operation with other support staff, ensure the availability of course materials; monitor students' performance, including their use of the library and other resources; be available to discuss study problems; obtain student feedback; liaise with members of staff and make arrangements for examinations and other student assessments.

What is needed is someone professionally competent in academic work to ensure high standards in what teachers regard as donkey work, and where, in practice, teaching often falls down. The work would not be only office work. Assistance in classrooms would be normal. We need to work towards a conception of course teams of, say, three or four academic staff and a course manager. Inevitably teams will vary in size, but they need to be small enough to be cohesive, yet large enough to contain a blend of talents.

Course managers might be fairly recent graduates of the same, or a closely related course, who have undertaken a year's training. This 'training' should include a training in production of teaching materials, curriculum design, teaching methods and methods of course evaluation. They should be familiar with the nature of professional development and the administration of student selection and asessment. The training should also include some shorthand and typing (shorthand for the meetings and typing for the course materials). An important element could be the development of skills in study counselling; but there are also arguments against this: it is probably asking too much of a one-year course and it is often better for study counsellors to be completely independent of the organization or the courses for which they are counselling.

It should be noticed that course managers do not have an official professional development role. They would not have sufficient experience for that and might have no experience of teaching at all. Nonetheless, if this proposal worked well, there would be an injection of educational knowledge into every working group. It remains to be seen what effect, if any, this might have. The effects are unlikely to be harmful; they may be beneficial in the long term. A pilot scheme would be worth trying.

The post of 'course manager' or 'course assistant' could be the first rung of a career in either teaching or administration in higher education. Both career paths would require further professional development. Course manager could also be the grade to which a long-serving, able and responsible departmental secretary aspires. The salary would be between the secretarial and lecturer grades. Because these posts could lead to academic careers, we should expect the grade to attract some young applicants of high intellectual ability, particularly at a time when recruitment to the academic professions is not fluent.

A proposal of this kind is bound to meet opposition. By taking duties previously performed by others, it is likely to cut across vested interests; and, since it is difficult to anticipate how the proposal would work in all its details, there would be initial objections that could only be answered by a pilot scheme.

Two objections stand out. One is that the attempt to improve teaching by inserting a new kind of efficiency and expertise at the bottom (while the provision for heads of department put forward in Proposition 5.6 creates a suitable climate from the top) could backfire if established staff now believe they can leave everything to the course manager. Secondly, it will be objected that any appointment to junior posts will necessitate retirements or redundancies of currently established staff. For this reason, and because like any new scheme it should first be piloted, the grade would only be introduced gradually (eg over a period of fifteen to twenty years). Because the salaries at this grade would be lower than those of established academics and administrators, the number of new posts should exceed the number they in effect replace.

It might be further objected that this work should be done by more senior staff who carry greater prestige. There is some truth in this, but it will depend upon the department. A mixture of junior and senior staff may be appropriate. Following the AUT/UAP Agreement in 1972, university departments are supposed to have appointed 'senior departmental colleagues' to help new staff, but they have not always pursued this responsibility diligently.

However, the proposals for course managers and senior staff both require some kind of provision for professional development to be made outside the institutions in which these staff work. It is to these arrangements we shall now turn.

PROPOSITION 6.0 THE CHANGES NEEDED REQUIRE A CENTRAL INITIATIVE.

This will be an unpopular proposal, particularly at this time. So sensitive are academic staff to any kind of external interference that it may be perceived as draconian.

The proposal being tentatively floated here is not for an organization with any kind of managerial role; but for a servant responding to demand. Indeed I have already argued that the basic social and working groups are, and will be, the major instruments of professional development (Proposition 3.2), that individuals should work with others to plan their own development (Proposition 5.3), that institutional policies should be formed to suit local circumstances, and so on. Professional development should emphatically not be promoted by a highly centralized or authoritarian system.

Nonetheless some professional development services cannot easily be provided within an institution and will need to be provided outside it. Notice that there is no reason why the professional development services provided outside an institution should be confined to the 'teaching function' of higher education. There are many other aspects of professional work that need development. Some of these were mentioned in Proposition 1.3.

The fact that institutions cannot themselves provide all the professional development services they need is not in itself a reason why the alternative provision needs be national or regional. It is not geography, but common needs that should bring institutions together. Nor should it be assumed that a supporting organization would necessarily need extensive central offices, a national staff college, or any other great expense characteristically associated with a central bureaucracy. Most of its activities will be in the institutions themselves and organized by their members.

However, there are powerful arguments for some kind of national arrangement and since the Committee of Vice-Chancellors and Principals has recently withdrawn financial support from its own national organization, the Co-ordinating Committee for the Training of University Teachers, it is now necessary to devote more space to these arguments than they would otherwise have received.

Proposition 6.1 A national body is needed to co-ordinate some aspects of professional development.

Proposition 6.1a Some professional development is best organized by an independent national body.

(i) The efficient use of limited expertise in professional development requires central co-ordination. Professional development, even when confined to the development of teaching, is a large field and there is no way that every institution could contain an expert on every part of it to a standard that is required when working with colleagues. For example, in some subjects it may be important to ensure that certain concepts are particularly well taught. To provide a course in the teaching of a specific concept, what is required is an information network to discover who is the best person in the country to provide it and then a central organization to arrange it.

Critics of a national organization will say that the benefits of its courses are not obvious. But that will not mean that there aren't any. One unfortunate difficulty is that when courses of this kind are successful hardly anyone notices the benefit. We only notice when things go wrong. When they go right, students do not finish their courses earlier; they will go on to other things. The average class of degree awarded does not suddenly rise. Institutions do not receive a financial bonus for being more efficient; and employers do not telegraph their congratulations. Although improvements have been made which may save hours of student frustration, institutions, and even the staff whose students improve, have no visible rewards for their respective expenditure and labour. Though the benefits are real, there are no immediate tangible incentives.

The malaise of contemporary teaching has its origins in the lack of rewards for improvements. The benefits of professional development, like the benefits of literacy, are slow, diffuse and yet bring profound cultural changes. The complexity of academic sub-cultures is such that neither the Treasury nor the Committee of Vice-Chancellors should always expect specifiable benefits as if benefits of education can be determined by some mechanistic process of cause and effect.

The point is that to expect professional development work to be able to demonstrate simple cause and effect in this way, and to finance it accordingly, is naïve. Decisions on the finance of the central co-ordination of professional development require more than administrative or political understanding. They require an understanding of human frailty. The improvement of teaching requires both the motivation and the means. The motivation I have considered elsewhere. The central provision of specialist professional development is one means.

(ii) There are other reasons for central co-ordination. I have already argued that it would be impolitic to organize courses for heads of departments within their own institutions. Courses or other activities organized in co-operation with external sponsors such as industrial companies, professional organizations, and international agencies, require a central person to act as link with over two hundred institutions of higher education. In particular, without some co-operation, it will be much more difficult to find support for research into professional development on a wide or national scale. This flaw could, in the long run, be fatal.

(iii) Thirdly, co-operation is needed to keep standards of examinations under constant review. Since the publication of the Robbins Report the number of qualifications, and the number of institutions giving apparently comparable qualifications, has risen dramatically. It may be a matter of opinion whether all degrees with the same label, such as BA, should represent the same standard (whatever that means), or whether there should be variable standards, as in the USA. Whatever policy is being adopted, we should know what it is, otherwise the currency is of doubtful value. Such safeguards are going to be of sudden importance with new patterns of courses, new curricula content, the expansion of continuing education, the introduction of credit transfer and increasingly open access. This is not an argument against such changes. It is a recognition that evaluation is a necessary concomitant of change. It may reasonably be objected that this is not a task for an organization primarily concerned with professional development. To some extent the CNAA already has this role. However there is virtually no provision for the systematic professional development of examiners and there ought to be.

Often, what is required is not a course, or 'training', but an opportunity to compare notes and share experiences. External examiners, for example, often have a solitary responsibility. A central agency could encourage such meetings and act as a convenor. There is an important role to be played by a central agency in giving trial scripts for parallel marking by new and more experienced examiners with the expectation that subsequent discussion will lead to professional development. The training of examiners is more feasible than the development of teaching skills and the effect of such training is more demonstrable. Yet remarkably little has been said about this need. If one asks 'why?' the answers inevitably reflect the cloak of secrecy which surrounds examining procedures.

Proposition 6.1b A central clearing house is needed for some kinds of professional development.

(i) In higher education there is constant duplication of effort. A great deal of time, effort and mistakes could be avoided if there were more fluent contact between institutions so that any academic could contact their counterparts by 'phone to discover how they have tackled particular problems, what difficulties they have encountered and how they have overcome them. The 'Contact' telephone information service based at Exeter and sponsored by the Council for Educational Technology has been a service of this kind.

(ii) There also needs to be a central clearing house so that industry and employers can make ready contact with specialists in particular areas of teaching and research. If such contacts were reciprocal, developments in research could be to the benefit of both.

(iii) Similarly, problems of staff immobility could be improved if there were a national clearing house to administer job exchanges, not only between institutions of higher education, but with other areas of employment. Experience between the civil sevice and industry shows that such a scheme is not without its difficulties, but that the benefits both for the employers and for the individual can be very worthwhile (Civil Service Dept. 1974).

(iv) The exchange of teaching materials also requires a central agency. With reductions in the numbers of academic staff, when many of them are teaching more or less the same thing in institutions all over the country, and when rapid technical developments have outstripped the educational expertise of audio-visual staff appointed in the immediate post-Robbins expansion, there is a need for a central agency to encourage the production of certain audio-visual material, to discourage duplication of effort, to provide up-to-date courses on modern techniques, to provide a 'Which?' guide to the purchase of equipment, to act as a clearing house for the dissemination of teaching materials, to exercise quality control by reviews and other conventional academic means and to ease the problems and expense of copyright. I particularly have in mind here the use of word processing facilities for the production of written scripts which can be modified for local use if the central agency copies and sends floppy discs to institutions in return for a fee. The advice, and possibly the co-operation, of the Council for Educational Technology and the British Library should be sought in this work. Within the field of professional development itself, the HERMES project has made important beginnings in the collection and dissemination of materials.

Admittedly, other organizations have attempted this role, but for various reasons they have not entered the lives of ordinary academics. For commercial companies the higher education market is too restricted. However mistakenly, the British Universities Film Council is seen as narrowly concentrating on film and as confining its attention to the universities. Too often materials do not demand sufficient activity from the student and they are frequently not adaptable to the orientation of particular courses.

The integration of a general service specifically for higher eduction, with wider issues in the development of teaching, should be to the benefit of both educational understanding and practice. General principles of teaching can be learned as a by-product of learning how to use specific materials. One role of a central agency is to make these principles explicit.

Proposition 6.1c But the need for systematic evaluation is not an argument for a central body.

In my view it is not necessary for a central body to act as an agency for evaluation of teaching and curricula. This is not because these roles will be confounded with its role in professional development. (Conflicting personal relationships and ambiguous roles arise when the same individual tries to do both jobs in a single institution; the same does not apply to an external institution with many individuals.) The reason is that these evaluations can be done in part by the CNAA, the UGC, the DES inspectorate or by some other system of external evaluators. Nonetheless, a national agency could play a part in clarifying criteria, developing techniques for evaluation and raising standards as part of its other activities.

Proposition 6.2 A co-ordinator is needed to service those with special responsibilities for professional development.

Proposition 6.2a 'Professional developers' also need to develop their skills.

The special difficulties of this work mean that those engaged in it also need to improve their skills in a conscious way. When professional developers were asked what issues and recommendations should be considered in this chapter, one wrote: 'We have a bad reputation for running events that are not particularly helpful, are not managed competently and do not meet needs or generate motivation. Courses should be arranged to provide "training" for all those who offer development activities. These courses should cover course planning, preparation and evaluation.' The Standing Conference on Educational Development Services in Polytechnics (SCEDSIP) and the Co-ordinating Committee for The Training of University Teachers (CCTUT) have already made important beginnings in this role. However the 'trainers' cannot be 'trained' in any didactic way. No approach is categorically best. Consequently the 'training' role for a co-ordinator requires considerable perspicacity. It needs to provide opportunities for self-directed professional development. These could include the organizaton of courses or the arrangement of meetings at which problems, insights, ideas and, most of all, approaches might be shared (cf Matheson 1981).

Proposition 6.2b Members of a co-operative group can give personal support for professional development.

A major need in professional development is emotional support for those engaged in it. For some people, particularly those who have no basic social and working group of their own, this work can be stressful. Any policy that extends responsibility for it risks increasing that stress rather than sharing it. In my opinion the CCTUT was quite correct when it saw part of its role as therapeutic (Matheson 1981, page 132).

Futhermore, it is not easy for those engaged in this work to explain the difficulty without seeming incompetent, disturbed or, by implication, accusing their colleagues. An authoritative external expert can do so. One of the roles of an inter-institutional agency is to establish mutually supportive working groups away from each individual's own institution.

Proposition 6.2c A national body is required to pursue research, and to disseminate knowledge on higher education, particularly that which is relevant to professional development.

By scholarship I mean the interpretation of existing knowledge, as distinct from the discovery of new knowledge by research. We saw in Proposition 4.4 that one reason for the lack of research into higher education is that few basic social and working groups exist to do this in higher education itself. In this respect higher education is unlike other fields. It does not have a body of students to be taught or to regenerate itself. Nor is there a career structure for researchers into higher education. Professional development work is the nearest thing to it.

A national body must not only promote the study of professional development and research into higher education, but strive for the academic recognition of these activities. Such activities are typical of other academic departments — the production of publications, attendance at seminars and conferences, etc. Where they differ is that while most academics form tight social and working groups and protect their boundaries from invasion, a national organization for professional development and professional developers in institutions would continually try to widen their boundaries to include members of other groups. Its ideal would be to circulate information to all groups, not only those actively engaged in professional development.

The Society for Research into Higher Education has actively pursued this role and no doubt any national body should work closely with it.

Proposition 6.2d A national body is required to keep the evaluation of professional development under review.

The evaluation of professional development is not the same as the evaluation of professional developers. It is not the role of a national body to undertake the formal evaluation of professional colleagues. That would conflict with its supportive role. But in keeping the evaluation of professional development under review, it should constantly gather information to inform its own provision, its support for others, and its promotion of professional development policies.

Formative evaluation of staff in professional development will be an on-going activity of professional development committees and others within each institution. It is not an easy task, and a national body could advise and disseminate information on how to do it. There is no reason why committees should not follow a similar procedure to that described under Proposition 5.5.

The success of professional development policies in an institution as a whole can be judged by reviewing changes in professional development plans from year to year, assuming the implementation of the suggestion for such plans made in Proposition 5.4.

Proposition 6.3 A national body is necessary to promote professional development policies.

Proposition 6.3a There needs to be a national focus for consensus on professional development issues.

There needs to be an organization that can from time to time present the collective view of professional developers or other staff. Of course if these two were to conflict, the body could become a forum to discuss opposing views and to reconcile them. While this would take professional development into the forefront of academic politics, and this may be a bad thing, it is inevitable if professional development is a constructive path to the future. Politics too is concerned with change.

There is a second, very different reason for requiring a focus for consensus. The improvement of professional development is a continual bootstrap operation. It is not a matter of gaining acceptability first and then introducing courses or other methods of training; these things must go together. The fear of professional development activities has to be overcome by the experience that there is nothing to fear. Professional development work is also a bootstrap operation in that the only way we can learn to do it is by doing it. For this reason we need an organization where ideas and experience can be shared.

If sharing is not national and across all sections of higher education, it is not complete. The sharing should also include drawing upon experience from other countries. Since, in some places, they have national bodies, liaison is better at the level of a national institution. If we had no national body such liaison could go by default. The testing of ideas may include trying out workshops and programmes in various contexts and subjecting them to the normal processes of academic judgement. The testing of programmes is critical in any new development. For example the development of courses for 'course managers' (call them what you please) will require special attention.

Proposition 6.3b Professional development needs national advocates.

A related point arises from the fact that professional developers are usually politically weak in their own institutions. Their difficulties are most unlikely to be overcome in all institutions by local efforts alone. There must be outside support. Ways must be found to make professional development more acceptable, not only to institutions but to individuals at the level of basic social and working group. For this many things are needed, of which one is political credibility within higher edcation. An organization which is not national is not likely to have sufficient clout.

Proposition 6.3c A national organization is needed to promote national policies for professional development.

A national body should use its political credibility and shared experience to promote national policies for professional development. This means it will need as many links as possible with teachers at the chalkface as well as members and representatives of other bodies. It also means that such a body will need to have long-term objectives, and long-term plans and methods to achieve them. Hence it should have a strategic role. To pursue this it will need personnel who combine vision with hard practicality. It will also need assured finance and the confidence of its sponsors. It is this that CCTUT lacked, in spite of its high level of activity and achievement with limited resources and severe constraints.

A national body could also have a role of advocacy with professional organizations outside higher education. For example, one concern of the authors of the curriculum chapter in the first SRHE Leverhulme volume on the teaching function is that some professional organizations can virtually dictate substantial parts of a department's curriculum (on pain of refusing professional recognition of courses) even though their members may have little educational expertise (Bligh 1982). By bringing together academics in a single field, the body could encourage not only agreed expression of their educational views, but the advancement of educational standards and understanding between professions. Of course many disciplines already have vocational organizations which can speak with a united academic voice through external professional organizations; but this is not true of all disciplines. In either case there are some advantages in being able to call upon independent educational expertise.

Any forms of professional development that require new forms of contract, or new kinds of incentive, will require consultations with unions and other bodies at a national level. For example, it would be advantageous for professional development and to increase staff mobility (with all the benefits that may result from that) if job exchanges between higher education and other sectors of employment were encouraged. While such a proposal could be, and has been, considered and proposed by other organizations, if it were advanced in the interests of professional development, a single national body for all higher education would be desirable to advance it. (The unions have other interests and do not form a single body.)

Proposition 6.3d Formal qualifications for teaching in higher education should be introduced when they could be acceptable.

When this suggestion has been mooted in the past it has been greeted almost with paranoia. Yet the reasons for it are the same as for other professions. They are principles on which the livelihood of many teachers in higher education depends. They are to do with the usefulness of knowledge, the value of theory and scholarship in their practical application, and the importance of feelings.

The time for this recommendation will come, but it is not yet. Research into higher education is insufficient (Proposition 4.4); the art of professional development is in its infancy (Proposition 4.5); and a professional qualification that is not accepted by the profession is of limited value.

Proposition 6.4 The establishment of a national organization for professional development across all higher education requires an initiative at government level.

Proposition 6.4a The decision to finance a national organization for professional development requires government initiative.

The idea of a national body is fraught with difficulties. One of these is the lack of incentives to use its service. Another lies in its finance.

The demands of autonomy may be satisfied by creating an opportunity with considerable incentives which individual institutions, or even individual members of staff, are free to take or refuse. When medical consultants attend some in-service courses, they are paid a notional sum equivalent to the fees they might have earned had they not attended. What is proposed here is something similar, except that the recompense should be made to the institution at a standard rate.

For example, a sum equivalent to a proportion of the salaries of each institution could be placed in a national trust fund. The trust could pay each institution sums not exceeding that proportion according to the time spent by their staff taking central courses or pursuing centrally organized activities. What the proportion should be depends upon what proportion of the academic's time should be spent on professional development activities outside his own institution. If an institution chose not to take advantage of the central provision, it would stand not to gain additional income for staff salaries.

It is not intended that any part of this sum should finance the national body. The national body would be financed by the interest upon it. Institutions will need to pay conference or course fees just the same as they do now, and in this way programmes organized centrally will be subject to market forces to ensure that they are run efficiently and in a cost-conscious manner.

Any organization, including the institutions themselves, students' unions and professional bodies, may make recommendations to the central body on the professional development activities which should be provided. For example, an institute of electrical engineering may recommend that special attention is given to the teaching of a new part of their subject. There could be more general courses on the marking of essays or the use of field work. No aspect of professional work should be excluded. At the time of writing the financing of the public sector of higher education seems likely to change. Consequently, the precise procedure recommended here will be subject to modification. Nonetheless, if the organization is to work across the whole of higher education, and much valuable experience would be lost if it did not, payments into the trust fund would need to be made early in the process of resource allocation — and this means at a governmental level.

The most important principle is that institutions should be paid a sum proportionate to the time that their staff spend on external professional development activities. A second principle is that the provision should be available to all sectors of higher education. A third is the freedom of individuals and their institutions to choose when and whether they will take advantage of the scheme. A fourth is the freedom to choose what provision they will patronize. And a fifth is their freedom to make recommendations on the provision made.

Proposition 6.4b The Department of Education and Science should establish a working party to consider the form, title, management and finance of a national organization for professional development in higher education.

It is not the purpose of this chapter to prescribe details of the national body on matters of its membership, staffing and finance. Nonetheless I will offer my preliminary thoughts.

I prefer the name 'Higher Education Development Council' indicating the wide spectrum of views that should be heard on it. The choice of membership is difficult in that a large number of bodies such as unions, student organizations, professional developers, employees from all sections of higher education, local education authorities, the UGC, special organizations such as the Council for Educational Technology, and many others might need to be represented on its governing board, or 'council'. On the other hand there is much to be said for those who are familiar with all the difficulties of professional development work having stronger influence. Just as institutional policies are torn between the needs of the institution and the personal needs of the individual, so, at a national level there is a tension between grassroots activity and political influence. My own preference is for a council with broad representation and a good number of practising professional developers, who will work through the establishment of small temporary working parties on which professional developers should normally be well represented. What must be avoided is a massive, inflexible organization.

Much of the purpose of the council would be to use the talents of individuals scattered throughout the country. Consequently, I do not envisage that it should have a large or permanent staff, but it should have money to commission specialists to perform chosen tasks. I imagine three, or possibly four, administrators each with secretarial support, working to sponsor the activities of an invisible college.

The council would hold large sums of money in trust and although the interest on these loans would vary greatly with the timing of income and expenditure, it would probably more than cover the costs even if interest rates were to fall well below their present levels.

However, I accept that there are difficulties on each of these points and for this reason I believe consideration by a working party would be the best way to resolve them. There are also serious value questions relating to institutional autonomy, the extent of academic freedoms, the rights of students and the reasonable expectations of the community as a whole.

CONCLUSIONS

The professional development of teaching in higher education is possible and important, but the task will be very difficult. We need to evolve totally new approaches to teaching with new support staff, new norms, new relationships, a different mix of students, including many from continuing education, new relationships to employment and new kinds of curricula. We need new standards of teaching.

The changes needed cannot take place quickly. Professional development will require planning and policies at an individual, institutional and national level. Any policies must recognize the suppressed feelings that professional development can arouse, the importance of incentives and research, the extent to which responsibilities for professional development at individual, departmental, institutional and national levels will in practice be exercised, and the need to evaluate and develop professional development itself.

REFERENCES

Black, P.J. and Sparkes, J.J. (1982) Teaching and learning. In Bligh, Donald (Editor) *Professionalism and Flexibility for Learning* Guildford: Society for Research into Higher Education

Bligh, Donald (Editor) (1982) *Professionalism and Flexibility for Learning* Guildford: Society for Research into Higher Education

Boud, D. and McDonald, R. (1982) *Educational Development through Consultancy* Guildford: Society for Research into Higher Education

Bramley, W. (1977) *Personal Tutoring* Guildford: Society for Research into Higher Education

Brown, G.A. (1977) Some myths of staff training and development *Impetus* 6, 2—8

Brown, G.A. (1978) *Lecturing and Exploring* Methuen

Brynmor Jones Report (1965) *Audio-visual Aids in Higher Scientific Education* London: HMSO

Chandler, E. (1977) *Student Counselling, When and Why?* Exeter University: Teaching Services

Civil Service Dept. (1974) *Report of the Task Force on Interchange of Scientists* London: HMSO

Civil Service Dept. (1976) *Progress Report on Interchange of Scientists and Engineers 1973—75* London: HMSO

Conrad, J. (1979) Denmark — the state of the art and the need for change. In Teather 1979 (pp. 87—105)

Cowan, J. (1977) Please try to understand our defence mechanisms *Impetus* 7, 30—33

Cox, R.J. (1967) Resistance to change in examining *Universities Quarterly* 21 (1) 35—38

Flood Page, C. (1975) Teasing hamsters in electric cages *Universities Quarterly* 29 (3) 318—331

Gibbs, G. (1982) The teaching function or the learning function. In Habeshaw, T. (Editor) (1982) *Three Ways to Learn* Standing Conference on Educational Development in Polytechnics

Greenaway, H.K. and Harding, A.G. (1978) *The Growth of Policies for Staff Development* Guildford: Society for Research into Higher Education

Hale Report (1964) *Report of the Committee on University Teaching Methods* London: HMSO

Halsey, A.H and Trow, M. *The British Academics* Faber and Faber

Harding, A.G., Kaewsonthi, S. and Roe, E. (1981) *Professional Development in Higher Education: State of the Art and the Artists* University of Bradford: Educational Development Service

Heron, J. (1982) *Education of the Affect — the unexplored domain* Bristol pre-seminar, Standing Conference on Educational Development Services in Polytechnics

Hewton, E. (1979) A strategy for promoting curriculum development in universities *Studies in Higher Education* 4 (1) 67—75

Hore, T. (1976) *The Political Situation of Teaching* Monash University: Advisory and Research Unit

Isaacs, G. (1979) Netherlands — Tertiary teacher training as a growth industry. In Teather 1979 (pp. 162—180)

Jalling, H. (1979) Sweden — strong central provision complementing local initiatives. In Teather 1979 (pp. 201—220)

Jalling, H. (1980) Educational policy and staff development. In Rhodes, D. and Hounsell, D. 1980 (pp. 31—38)

Katz, J. and Hartnett, T. (1976) *Scholars in the Making* Ballinger

King, M. (1973) The anxieties of university teachers *Universities Quarterly* 28 (1) 69—83

McMillan, J.H. (1975) The impact of instructional improvement agencies in higher education *Journal of Higher Education* Jan-Feb, 17—23

Main, A. (1980) *Effective Studying* Scottish Academic Press

Malleson, N.B. (1962) *The Influence of Emotional Factors on Achievement in University Education* Second Bartholemew Lecture and Sociological Review Monograph, Keele University

Malleson, N.B. (1967) Students leaving mechanical engineering courses *Universities Quarterly* 22 (1) 74—78

Marris, P. (1964) *The Experience of Higher Education* Routledge & Kegan Paul

Matheson, C.C. (1979) *The Workshop Way* Co-ordinating Committee for the Training of University Teachers

Matheson, C.C. (1981) *Staff Development Matters* Co-ordinating Committee for the Training of University Teachers

Mechanic, D. (1978) *Students under Stress* University of Wisconsin Press

Nuffield Group for Research and Innovation in Higher Education (1973—5) Newsletters 1—7

Parlett, M. (1978) The department as a learning milieu *Studies in Higher Education* 2 (2) 173—181

Phillips, S. (1979) Programmes and practitioners: We do what we are *POD Quarterly* 1 (2) 96—106

Raaheim, K. and Wankowski, J. (1981) *Helping Students to Learn at University* Sigma Forlag

Rhodes, D. and Hounsell, D. (1980) *Staff Development for the 1980s — international perspectives* Illinois State University Foundation and University of Lancaster

Robbins, Lord (1963) *Higher Education* London: HMSO

Rutherford, D. (1982) Institutional strategies for staff development: an analysis of four models *British Journal of Educational Technology* (in press)

Saunders, et al. (1969) *Report of the Commission on Teaching in Higher Education* National Union of Students

Sayer, S. (1977) Development and discourse *Impetus* 7, 34—36

Shore, B.M. (1979) Canada — an emphasis on instructional development. In Teather 1979 (pp. 56—86)

SRHE (1982) The research career *SRHE Bulletin* 113

Still, R.J. (1963) *Psychological Illness among Students in the Examination Period* Leeds University: Department of Student Health

Teather, D.C.B. (1979) *Staff Development in Higher Education: An international review and bibliography* Kogan Page

Wankowski, J.A. (1973) Educational counselling: a helping hand in restoring shattered learning competence *Proceedings of the British Student Health Association* 25

Wheeler, M. (1982) *Counselling in Study Methods* Exeter University: Teaching Services (in press)

ACKNOWLEDGEMENTS

Professional development is a controversial subject and there are very diverse opinions about it. Being aware of my own bias, but not perhaps my own prejudices, when preparing this chapter I sought the opinions of a large number of people actively interested in professional development in higher education. I am greatly indebted to them for broadening my horizons and regret that not all their views could be included. Their names are listed below. I asked them first what issues should be considered in this paper, and then what recommendations they thought should be made. Professor Lewis Elton helped me classify the issues they submitted. Not surprisingly my first attempts to combine their recommendations did not produce a very digestible or well documented paper! I have subsequently benefited from detailed comments by Dr William Taylor, Professor John Cowan, Dr Sinclair Goodlad, Jessica Claridge and members of the pre-seminars convened by Dr Alex Main in Strathclyde and Dr David Armstrong in London. To all of them I am most grateful, but responsibility for the paper is mine.

Dr J. Abercrombie, Professor R. Atkinson, Mr G. Badley, Dr. F. Bell, Mr N. Boreham, Dr G. Brown, Mr B.S. Cane, Mr K. Challinor, Mr J.L. Clarke, Mr R. Clayton, Dr E. Cope, Dr J. Cowan, Mr S. Cox, Mr C. De Winter Hebron, Dr A. Digby, Mr G.D.C. Doherty, Mr A.J. Dunk, Mr D. Edynbry, Dr C. Evans, Mr L. Evans, Mr R.G. Farmer, Miss P. Fleetwood-Walker, Dr. D. Fox, Mr K.L. Gardner, Mr G. Gibbs, Mr R. Glanville, Mr B. Gomes da Costa, Dr. B. Greaves, Dr A.G. Harding, Dr E.S. Harri-Augstein, Dr R.D. Harrison, Professor D.G. Hawkridge, Mr R.L. Helmore, Dr E. Hewton, Miss B. Hollinshead, Miss G. Hood, Mr D. Hounsell, Mr B. Jones, Mr H. Jones, Mr H.T. Jones, Mr J. Konrad, Dr R. McAle, Mr J. McCann, Dr G.P. McGregor, Mr P.C. McNaught, Dr D. Mack, Dr A. Main, Dr C.C. Matheson, Dr D.J. Mortimer, Mr A.L. Nicholas, Dr C.R. Palmer, Dr P.K. Poppleton, Mr D.F.L. Pritchard, Dr J. Richardson, Mr R. Roberts, Dr D. Rutherford, Miss S. Sayer, Mr G. Settle, Miss K.M. Simmonds, Dr G.J. Stodd, Dr K. Swinhoe, Dr L. Taylor, Professor P. Thody, Dr L.F. Thomas, Dr P. Toyne, Dr S. Trickey, Mr R.E. Wakeford, Mr D. Warren Piper, Dr G.M. Wilkinson.

3

THE VALUES PRESUPPOSED

by Mary Warnock

The title of this chapter is manifestly, almost disgracefully, general. Not only does the subject matter underlie all the contributions to the SRHE Leverhulme volumes on the teaching function, but, embarrassingly, it equally flows over into the subjects of all the other volumes in the series. In particular it seems to me impossible to discuss values and goals in anything other than a vacuously abstract way without reference to the binary system of higher education, as we confusedly have it in this country. If life were tidy this topic would be saved up for the last volume (on the future) or that and the last but one (on structure and governance). But it cannot be avoided at this stage of the series. People frequently refer to the problems of the binary system, its original aims, what was intended by it, whether it works. But this talk is itself value-laden, and presupposes a good many assumptions about what we *want* from our total system of higher education. Therefore in this discussion of values, in which I hope to expose for further discussion *some* (but not all) of the values assumed in the earlier contributions, I find I cannot altogether avoid a discussion of the system as a whole. With this apology. I shall plunge straight into it.

THE FUTURE OF THE BINARY SYSTEM
In the case of secondary education, the structure of the provision as a whole is constantly discussed and is seen by everyone to be a question not merely of expediency or convenience but of values. The same kind of discussion should go on in the field of higher education. If we are to debate the teaching function of institutions of higher education, then it is essential that we should clarify our views about whether or not the teaching function is to be broadly the same in all the institutions with which we are concerned. And if it is not, then we should decide whether, as has been suggested, a statement of the different aims and a serious attempt at demarcation of different goals should be undertaken. It is for this reason that I shall put forward, in this section, two possible pictures of the future, and sketch some of the consequences likely to flow from working towards the actualization of each. Thus I hope I shall bring out some of the value concepts implicit in each programme.

Picture One: the Binary System Embraced
On this hypothesis, we do not merely accept the binary system, different funding and all, as an historical accident, the consequences of which we have

got to live with, but we *believe in it*, as a source of variety and flexibility within the whole provision of higher education. The original introduction of the system, after all, was not accidental, or only partially so. The white paper setting it up appeared in 1966. Speaking of it in 1971, Anthony Crosland, who was its originator, said (Boyle and Crosland 1971, p. 194): 'I became a passionate believer in Binary and Polytechnics, and I suppose did as much as anyone else to push the policy through'; and, explaining his enthusiasm, he said: 'Of those who are going on (to higher education) not all want a university type of education. Both the demand and the need is for pluralism, not a unitary system of Higher Education, and for alternative institutions which offer something totally diferent from the traditional universities.' He went on to quote Tyrrell Burgess on the need for institutions which cater 'not only for the traditional full-time degree courses but for the part-time student, the sub-degree course and the kind of education which has its roots in the technical college tradition.'

The advantages of such a system, then, seemed originally to be that the two types of institution would be truly different. Their different sources of finance seemed almost irrelevant: to be funded by local authorities was indeed part of the technical college tradition, but the important thing was the different 'type' of education on offer. Even if central funding had been chosen for all institutions, in Crosland's eyes there would still have been a need for two 'types'. The polytechnics were to offer education which was primarily technological; and they, unlike universities, were to be flexible about entry requirements, and about part-time and adult students.

At the time of Crosland's quotation, Tyrrell Burgess had not yet, obviously, had time to observe academic drift. Suppose that this had never occurred (as we cannot doubt that it has) would we have been prepared to agree with Crosland? Let us imagine a network of polytechnics existing alongside the universities, and offering education primarily in applied science and technology, but with other predominently practical courses as well, such as managerial courses and interpreters' courses. If it had worked, a number of problems would have solved themselves. The overall goal of 'pursuit of excellence' would have been common to all institutions of higher education, but new and innovatory teaching could have been introduced in the polytechnics, with no threat to old standards of scholarship. The market could have determined (give or take a bit) what courses to provide. The criterion of success, in any course, would have been the market demand for the product, the engineer or biological technician or whatever it was. New and workable links could have been forged between the polytechnics and both industry and the professions. Sandwich courses, post-experience courses, part-time and evening courses could all have been arranged.

The balance between research and teaching would equally, I suspect, have been settled. The primary purpose of the polytechnics must undoubtedly have been to teach. Good polytechnics would manage to provide time and facilities, through sabbatical leave and other means (including part-time teaching), for research to continue, and would have encouraged, in particular, research into teaching methods as well as the proper evaluation of courses. But teaching would still have come first.

Most important of all, I am inclined to think that, provided the polytechnics were truly esteemed for what they were doing (and you will remember that we have imagined away 'institutional academic drift'), the very existence of a different and competing system might galvanize the universities into improving their own standards, not of scholarship, but of teaching and, in general, of relations between staff and pupil. Universities, to put it crudely, would have been shamed into improving their techniques, and seeing to it that their students left having had the kind of education they wanted. They would not have been able to dismiss any concern with teaching skills as something fit only for the polytechnics. They would have realized that, if they were not careful, they would lose, not their worst, but their best students to the polytechnics, if the reputation of each kind of institution, though different, was equal. Rather as the BBC's television output was infinitely improved in the 1950s by the advent of a competing system, so the universities might well have benefited.

But even at the beginning, some people were sceptical about whether this would work. Edward Boyle, also talking to Maurice Kogan in 1971 (op. cit., p. 128) said:

> 'There's no easy solution to this problem of the binary system. I feel that out-and-out critics of the system tend to overlook two key points. First, how much research should be undertaken in polytechnics and colleges of education, and of what kind? It couldn't be sensible to try to replicate research which is already being undertaken in universities. Secondly, how much are we prepared to spend on building up the libraries of what are called the "non-autonomous" institutions so that they approximate to university standards? It's no use shirking such questions. ...The binary system as we have it today is unstable.'

Boyle's point was that even if one accepted the binary system, it might be unrealistic to suppose that it could continue as it started. He said: 'I think a policy of the DES saying to the polytechnics "Whatever you do, we must build you up and you must keep your distance from the universities" is very much more schematic than real. Any attempt at precise articulation of the difference between what a university is for and what a polytechnic is for won't stand up.' He went on to say that the real difference lay in the amount of money available to each type of institution for research. Both were interested in teaching, but the work of a university as opposed to a polytechnic could be summed up as *teaching within an atmosphere of research.*

Now this is, it seems to me, a percipient thought, and an attractive one. But it also seems to contain all the seeds of the lack of stability that Boyle himself foresaw; and indeed it foreshadows all the difficulties that lie in the way of embracing the binary system with enthusiasm. For our present hypothesis, that the system be welcomed and exploited for its own sake and for the sake of the benefits it can bring, is entirely dependent upon our presumption that one can imagine away 'academic drift'. And to say this is to say that one can positively imagine what used to be called parity of esteem existing between the universities and the polytechnics. It is odd that Anthony Crosland, who was such a fierce critic of a secondary education system that attempted to divide schools into grammar schools and secondary modern, should have argued that the dual system at the level of higher education was not only defensible but positively desirable and necessary. For difficulties of a precisely parallel kind seem to be built into it; and unless there could be genuine equality of respect for both kinds of institutions then none of the good consequences we have imagined could follow. There could be no allocation of functions between the two, no distribution of curriculum, no sharing of facilities, no genuine planned acceptance of the different roles of the two sides of the divide. But is it possible that such acceptance could ever come about, as long as the disparity between the resources for research remained? If we think that it could not really happen, then perhaps we should turn to the other hypothesis.

Picture Two: the Binary System Abolished
Throughout all the SRHE Leverhulme papers we have before us, the attempt has been made to talk about higher education as a whole, and indeed the purpose of the series of conferences has been to survey and to discuss higher education without special reference to where it is carried out. If such an attempt is feasible at all, then it looks as if most people actually want higher education to be at least partially unified. It makes no sense to discuss the role of teachers, the methods of changing the curriculum, the aims and techniques of student assessment, how to recruit and to encourage staff over the whole system, if there is a radically different task to be performed by the universities from the task of the local authority-funded institutions. No one has said, for example: 'Let continuing education be allocated to the polytechnics and colleges.' No one has said: 'Let polytechnics concentrate on teaching undergraduates, and leave research and the teaching of graduates to the universities.' It seems that the case is as Edward Boyle said it was: there are no intelligible differences of aim between the two sides of the divide. If we want parity of esteem, and a rational distribution both of students and of resources, and above all if we want a sensible, economical and mutually agreed specialization in the institutions we are talking about, so that futile reduplication is avoided, then surely the best way to achieve this is by the radical step of abolishing the different funding, and hence the different status, of the two kinds of institutions. It is of course difficult to say very much in detail about such a plan at the present time, when the whole question of funding of the polytechnics is under review.

But it is at least possible to talk about it in general terms. What would, broadly speaking, be the consequences of unification?

One point is by now obvious. When we talk about higher education we essentially believe that this cannot be divorced from research. This point will come up again and again. We have already seen that if universities are acknowledged to be the only serious centres of research, then the parity of esteem needed to make the binary system as good as it was supposed to be simply will not exist. If the binary system were abolished, it would be presumed that research went on in all institutions, and people would undertake research indifferently according to where the necessary libraries of laboratories or other resources were. Institutions would be specialist, to a certain extent, as they are now. But there could be more rationality in the recognition and growth of specialization. To make such comparison feasible, and to ensure the standards were maintained overall, there would be the need, as there is now, for peer assessment of the departments in different institutions, through the agency of the research councils. But, given this, the fertilization of one institution by another would be infinitely easier. And this is something which has an acknowledged value. At present the complications of a different salary structure and different pension schemes alone make it almost as difficult to change from working in a university to a polytechnic, or the other way round, as it is to change from higher to secondary teaching.

But the main and most desirable consequence of this radical abolitionist plan is simply that it would fulfil, in the only logical way, the aims already implicit in the awarding of *degrees* by polytechnics (and colleges) as well as by universities. The concept of radically different *kinds* of degree-giving institutions simply seems absurd. There would be great satisfaction in abolishing it at a stroke.

The only drawback that I can see is, in fact, a fatal one. It would not work. Even if the source of funding of all institutions of higher education could be unified, this would not actually bring about uniformity of any more genuine kind. This is a matter of history and, as we all know, one cannot rewrite history, or not in a day. But, more important, do we want to? One of the features of any institution, school, business, or university which causes it to be a success rather than a failure is the loyalty of its members. This is a truth often repeated, but still worth thinking about. I want now to make a brief digression to say something about the immense differences that exist within the university system itself, which would in my view make it hard enough to treat all universities as running on the same lines. If what I suggest is true, then it would be even more difficult to envisage a time when all the disparate institutions of higher education could come to think of themselves as basically unified in one system.

I make this digression with some hesitation, but largely because in the two SRHE Leverhulme volumes on the teaching function I see very little reflection of the differences between different institutions. I believe that the desire for uniformity, or more politely, equality, has to some extent overcome accuracy, so that differences have been somehow ironed out (and this is odd in one sense, because freedom to follow one's own path is also one of the values most obviously accepted in these two volumes. But we shall come on to this later).

Within the university sector, then, the major difference I see, and it is not a trivial one, is between a truly collegiate university and one which is not collegiate but monolithic. This difference is reflected in almost all the aspects of academic life discussed in these two volumes. It is reflected in the relation between teaching and research, in the relation between both of these and administration, in the relation between teacher and pupil, and between one member of staff and another. To start at the beginning, at Oxford and Cambridge, though there are minimum university entrance requirements, it is the colleges and not the university faculties which select students (with a few exceptions in the case of very small schools). The colleges can, if they wish, specialize in certain subjects, and not accept candidates in others. Their overall numbers are now limited, but they can fill the places they have as they wish and as suits their teaching capacity. Fellows of colleges, whether tutorial fellows who do most of the teaching, or research fellows, are not employed by their colleges; they are their colleges. The word 'staff', unqualified, in Oxford means the college servants. Many tutorial fellows stay as tutorial fellows all their working life; and many of them wish to do exactly that. They fit their research round their teaching. The whole question of 'promotion' looms far less large in a collegiate university. There are, of course, professors and readers who, while remaining professorial fellows of colleges, are wholly paid by the university, and they have responsibility for their departments and for the admission, and much of the supervision, of graduates. But such jobs are not always sought after. As to the administration, fellows administer their own colleges, and some of them take their turn at administering the university. Some become relative specialists in that line. But it is seldom a matter of great competition.

The notion of being first and foremost a member of a college has various consequences, not least for the relation between fellows and undergraduates. Rightly or wrongly, though colleges co-operate with each other, they are also in competition with each other. So if I, as a member of my college, have selected a certain undergraduate, it is because I want him as a member of my college. I want him to do well, not only for his sake but for mine. I want the reputation of my college to stand high, not only academically, but on the less measurable scale of being a place where people enjoy themselves, of which they are glad to be a member. All this imperceptibly encourages a fairly close interest in undergraduates among at least a high proportion of fellows. And colleges are small enough to make this possible.

I am not saying that all these things are good, though I suspect that they mostly are; and I am certainly not saying that when we come to the question of curriculum, or teaching methods, the collegiate universities are impeccable — far from it. I am at this stage simply suggesting that it is extraordinarily difficult to say anything useful about the values and aims, still less about the methods and the curriculum, of all universities, when there are such vast differences between them, only one, though a major one, of which I have mentioned. How much more difficult is it, then, to include in a generalization all the polytechnics and colleges of higher education as well.

Though Edward Boyle was probably right, then, and the binary system is intrinsically unstable, perhaps this is no bad thing. Though we may not be able to articulate coherently different aims and purposes for the different sides of the great divide, it may be that the historical origins and the development of different institutions, whichever side of the divide they fall, generate their own aims and purposes. One of the value questions we have to try to answer is *whether we want this pluralism to continue or whether we don't*. This is why I have here formulated the two hypotheses.

THE CURRICULUM
The second part of this chapter is concerned with the absolutely central questions *What should be taught? and how should it be taught?* Of the topics which cluster round these two questions, the second is perhaps less controversial. It would be generally agreed that teaching is often less than satisfactory at present. But it can hardly be improved in isolation from consideration of what is to be taught. A curriculum which satisfied the demands of higher education should generate its own teaching successes.

At the beginning of this section, I must reiterate what are my own considerable doubts about the utility of dealing with the higher education sector as a whole, especially when the subject matter under discussion is the curriculum. The analogy to notorious questions about the length of a piece of string seem obvious. A hint of these doubts is expressed at the beginning of the specific chapter on the curriculum in the first SRHE Leverhulme on the teaching function (Bligh 1982), but the doubts are nevertheless put on one side. It may be that this calls in question the validity of the recommendations of that chapter. If I personally seem to be speaking in a somewhat élitist or ivory tower tone, that is perhaps because I genuinely cannot believe that all institutions of higher education can or should offer the same kind of courses or cater for the needs of the same kind of student, and I make no pretence of speaking of that of which I have only second-hand knowledge. It is worth saying this, because I suspect that a good deal of fruitless discussion might result from a failure to recognize the differences to which I tried to call attention in the first part of my chapter.

With that warning in mind, let us nevertheless try to see what values the recommendations contained in the curriculum chapter reflect (and many of these values are equally expressed, as one would expect, in the papers on teaching and on continuing education and on the developing of staff competence).

Social Accountability
Perhaps more prominent than anything else seems to be the demand for social accountability. Just as the old Reithian ideas which lay behind the early days of the BBC have been gradually eroded, so that, increasingly, the broadcasting authorities are now supposed not only to serve, but also to reflect the needs of the community, and to give the community what it wants and can demand, so the concept of the university as dictating to society, determining for itself what degree courses there shall be, and what shall be their content, is gradually withering away. The potential conflict between the ideal of 'accountability' and the ideal of freedom is something we shall discuss later. For the time being, let me say that I suppose accountability to entail a concept of justification by an institution to society at large, or, ultimately, to parliament. This justification may take the form (as with public companies) of a mere obligation to publish accounts, with a description each year of the activities and prospects of the company. On the other hand it may suggest, as I think the phrase 'social accountability' does suggest, that people in general have not only a right to know what goes on, but a right to be satisfied with it. Nevertheless social accountability is not itself a wholly unambiguous concept. In the simplest sense (a) it may suggest that a university is under an obligation to demonstrate, with regard to all of its courses, that they have a recognizable social utility. This would be easy in the case of those courses directly related to issues on which the public at large feels strongly; thus medical and paramedical courses, courses in veterinary sciences and engineering, courses, somewhat paradoxically, which led to teaching qualifications, even courses in arts subjects, would all be easy to justify. Other courses would be less easy, but with a certain amount of care, a good deal of relatively 'pure' research could be made acceptable, and so could the teaching of foreign languages and even some kinds of social and political theory. But (b) a more Aristotelian view of the relation between universities and society could be envisaged. It could be argued that a society would prefer to *see itself in the position of having a leisured, cultivated, and highly educated class;* and that the better the society, the larger the class of those interested in culture and leisure would be. Aristotle graded states according, more or less, to the number of people they contained who could enjoy 'schole' — cultivated leisure in which to peruse the pleasures of philosophy and pure speculation. It is not a bad kind of scale, especially if it is extended to include leisure for the enjoyment and the pursuit of the pleasures of the arts. On this broad and humane view of society (admittedly more suitable for a time of prosperity than for

the present day) the task of justifying university activities to society will be very much easier.

The question may be put thus: are we being told (a) that universities should adapt themselves to society and adopt the values of that society whatever they may be? (and here it is necessary to remember that, as Randolph Quirk pointed out in *The Times* of 2 February this year, society shows itself fairly indifferent to the fate of its universities, and even those who are old members of universities are not often prepared to speak up for them). Or is it (b) that universities should expect that society would adapt to them, in a co-operative effort to civilize and improve the life of that society as a whole? To argue for the second relationship is perhaps to look back to a society rather like that of, say, Edinburgh in the eighteenth or even the nineteenth century when universities were especially revered. But it is not an impossible mode.

The Practical Element
Secondly, and not unconnected with the former point, there is considerable demand in the SRHE Leverhulme volumes on the teaching function not only for social relevance in university courses, but also for a practical element. The opposite of practice is of course theory. It may be that the demand for practice could therefore best be satisfied by the teachers' constant vigilance that students keep their eyes partly on the present state of the world (including the up-to-date world of scholarship and research); and that they, the teachers, should be aware of the need to discipline their students to write and speak in a way that would be intelligible and explanatory to people in the world outside the university. The demand for practicality, in this sense, seems not only sensible in the light of the previously discussed demand for accountability, but it is also very much in accord with the noticeable trend in political theory and philosophy, to mention only two of what have sometimes in the past been highly theoretical subjects.

On the other hand, in the chapter on the curriculum, much more appeared to be envisaged, including periods of work for all students in hospitals or schools or factories. I am fairly certain that at this point we have come up against one of the areas where to generalize over the whole field of higher education is not helpful. That there should be some sandwich courses, some thick and some thin sandwiches, that there should be some courses a precondition of the entry for which should be work experience, could not I think be seriously disputed. But whether it makes sense to demand such mixed courses universally over the whole field is far more dubious (and I do not mean merely to call attention to the fact that such a scheme would be expensive and time-consuming, especially for the receiving institutions).

An Ambiguous Attitude to Scholarship
The demand for practice as well as theory goes along with an extremely ambiguous attitude in more of the chapters than one towards scholarship. A good deal is said about the need to ensure that whatever happens to our institutions, academic standards are preserved. But it is less than clear what is entailed in this. Part of the ambiguity here is caused, I think, not so much by the attempt to treat all higher education as one, as by the failure to differentiate between the sciences and the humanities. In the sciences we are accustomed to drawing a distinction between pure and applied science, and especially between research that is directed towards some specific need or problem, and fundamental research. The demand, in curriculum terms, seems to be that undergraduates should not be expected to go further into pure or theoretical science than will enable them to turn their attention more intelligently to the applied aspects of their study, and its potential relevance to social needs. Equally, at the graduate level, there is once again a debate between those who advocate more 'applied' research, and those who fear this. The thinking behind this is partly a perfectly general wish that undergraduate studies should not be too specialized, partly the presumption that only exceptional students are going to proceed to research. There is an enormous majority of average students in higher education who need to make themselves practically and intelligently employable in the real world. The demand for this kind of 'balanced' curriculum in the sciences gives rise to many of the demands for teaching of a practical, intelligible, relatively down-to-earth kind. The horror stories from physics students reinforce this very proper demand: let teachers, once a balanced curriculum has been decided upon, get on and ensure that their pupils actually learn what they have to learn in order to progress along the syllabus-route in an orderly fashion. Many subject syllabuses, after all, are naturally progressive. You have to have mastered part one before moving on to part two. This is not a matter of decision on anyone's part, but of necessity, like learning the elementary parts of mathematics before the more advanced, or learning four-part harmony before six part.

It is very difficult to transfer this sort of thinking into the area of the humanities; and in particular the distinction between 'pure' and 'applied', between 'fundamental' and 'problem-orientated' research, seems to sit rather uneasily on the actual practice of undergraduate and graduate students, and of their teachers. 'Scholars' are, more or less, those who go in for 'pure' or 'fundamental' research; and the curriculum demand equivalent to that which we have noticed among the scientists is the demand that students should not all be assumed to be 'scholars', but should be given a broad and general humanities course, geared somehow to the present day. For there is a common assumption, especially among scientists, that the scholarly is to be identified with the historical. Thus the scholarly linguist is the one who pores over ancient texts in High

German or Classical Chinese; the scholarly sociologist is the one who discovers about familial linkages in medieval Serbia. There is of course a certain truth in this. For it would be generally agreed among practitioners in the humanities that you cannot altogether understand any phenomenon, literary, artistic or social, without knowing something of its origins. And it follows that all those working in the humanities to some extent ride on the back of the historians. Therefore a system of higher education needs essentially, and not just accidentally, to perpetuate the practice of good historical research. But we should realize that to say this is precisely to say that scholarship is useful, indeed necessary, for any serious work in the humanities at all. It is not just an optional extra. Moreover, there is a kind of scholarship which is not historical at all, but which involves knowing a lot about and understanding the ramifications of a contemporary phenomenon. That there must be historians of language for the study of linguistics to be properly pursued, for example, does not entail that every student of linguistics must be an historian. And a particular linguistician, even a whole syllabus in linguistics, can well be scholarly without being historical. The opposite of 'scholarly' is not 'contemporary' but 'superficial'. Research then in this sense of 'scholarly', must be scholarly if it is to be worth pursuing. But to say that research is worth pursuing, whether in the humanities or the sciences is not to say either that it is worth pursuing 'for its own sake' or 'for the benefits it will bring'. It may well be worth pursuing in both ways; equally it may be impossible to tell, at the beginning, which way it will be worth pursuing, or whether it will be worth pursuing at all.

Behind all the confusions, then, about 'pure' and 'applied', 'fundamental', 'scholarly' and so on, there lies in our volumes a very proper sense that without research, higher education could not go on. All the curricula in higher education must be constructed in so open-ended a way that they can flow into research, and the results of research can flow back into them. So much I believe is common ground. And it is this ground that underlies the attempt to treat all higher education, wherever it is carried on, as ultimately one kind of education, rather than, on the Crosland pattern, as divided into different types. Nevertheless, there is clearly a tension between what is felt to be the need of ordinary undergraduate students to be taught to understand their subject as a whole, and the need for subjects, of their own momentum, to become more and more 'difficult', whether the difficulty lies in their becoming more theoretical or more detailed and intricate — more demanding of 'scholarship'.

An Ambiguous Attitude to Specialization
This leads, finally, to the ambiguous attitude in the volumes to specialization for students. There is a plaintly articulated demand that the entry requirements for candidates for higher education should be less

specialized. But more controversially, there is, incorporated in the curriculum chapter the radical suggestion that undergraduate courses should last for two years only, and be 'general'. Specialization would then follow for selected students, whose speciality would be determined by where there was a 'need for specialists'. This is filled out by the suggestion that the overall balance in curriculum objectives over higher education as a whole should be reflected in the curriculum followed by each individual student. If I understand this suggestion rightly, it means that if we believe in the value of having courses in geography and languages and biochemistry and engineering, within the system as a whole, then not only should each institution have such courses on offer, but each student should build up for himself a curriculum out of 'modules' from all these different disciplines. Just as the good secondary school urges its pupils to take 'O' levels in a wide range of different subjects, both so that they may have a broad general knowledge of a range of things, and also may keep their options for later specialization open for as long as possible, so, we are told, in universities also there should be balanced curricula, looking towards specialization for some at a later stage, but functioning as a good end-point of education for the majority, who will leave without proceeding to the next stage. The 'O' level model, if we may call it that, has the added advantage that it should be easier for adult students to take parts of it, add up credits, educate themselves part-time, and follow courses leading to the examinations but perhaps through distance learning.

In considering these proposals it seems to me that we need very carefully to consider *the arguments in favour of 'breadth'*. Is it desirable that students who are by now in most senses grown-up, should be obliged by the system to continue to study subjects in which they have perhaps no particular interest, (and this question would be even more pressing if specialization at school were diminished). Is there not perhaps a time when the freedom of the student to follow his own interests should be allowed priority, within the constraints of what the higher education system as a whole has to offer? Ought we totally to discount the pleasures of abandoning some subjects and concentrating on others? Nor is this point wholly answered by those who would interpret 'breadth' to mean not so much a taste of this and that in modules, but rather an insistence on interdisciplinary work. Not all those who study both ancient history and philosophy want to be compelled to study the relationship between them; and it is in practice extraordinarily difficult to get interdisciplinary courses decently taught, even in joint seminars.

But to return to the modular at the level of experience, it is moreover necessary to look at the practical disadvantages which have been found in some ambitious modular courses in polytechnics. Increasingly it is found that students cannot, in fact, choose their modules freely, but are constrained by the demands of certain linear subjects, where they cannot take, let us say, the option in biochemistry without first taking that in chemistry, nor the option in Baroque opera without first taking the basic musicianship course. And so an old-style curriculum tends to build up, but in a somewhat random way. If it is argued that this need not be so, that were the modular components better thought out they could be conceived as free-standing, then the drawback becomes different. It turns out that all of the modules are pitched at the same level of difficulty, so that the work a student does in his second year is no different in style from that which he did in his first year. This is, I believe, a real point of conflict. There are values here which must urgently be discussed. Could we satisfy ourselves that a student had advanced, that he had changed intellectually in the way that I suppose many think that he should change in going through a course on higher education, if after three years (or two, on the proposed curriculum paper scheme) he could tackle only the same kind of courses as he tackled at the beginning? The charge of superficiality would now be hard to rebut. This charge is reinforced by the consideration that employers at the present time understandably prefer graduates who have followed naturally coherent courses, taking only those modules which are relevant to one another. Thus, for example, at Oxford Polytechnic, the employment prospects of those students who study dietetics and chemistry are far higher than of those who study dietetics and, say, English literature.

There is, however, another concept perhaps ultimately more fruitful than that of 'breadth', which is emphasized in at least two of the chapters here (on curriculum and on teaching), but which may well be thought to be implicit in all of them, and that is the idea that students in higher education should be *self-conscious about what they are doing and what they are doing it for*. Speaking of the desirability of problem solving as a means of teaching, the authors of the curriculum chapters say this:

> 'Students' work is often based upon essay writing which in turn often involves the assaying or testing of propositions. ...What is perhaps needed is a more self conscious and systematic celebration of these dimensions of study, a deliberate unveiling of these elements of the "hidden curriculum".'

I believe that this paragraph is of the greatest importance. It encapsulates, I think, the truth in the cliché (rightly taken as something to be used with caution, in the chapter on teaching) that students must be taught to think. It may sound paradoxical to speak of revealing the hidden curriculum. But the point is that students, as opposed to children, ought not unwittingly to be subject to a hidden curriculum. Moreover, when the teacher believes in the value of what he is doing, he has not only a right but a positive duty to explain to his pupil the respect in which he thinks it is valuable. If we go further into the case of essay-writing, this becomes clear. Students, especially in their first year, often regard the task of writing their essay as something arbitrarily imposed on them by 'the system' or even by the particular whim of their tutor. If they fail to write an essay, they apologize, as if they have either failed to conform to a pointless rule, or somehow done an injury to the tutor. It is very difficult for tutors to explain to their pupils what the point of the whole exercise is; but I think they ought to try. In this way they will be justified in demanding an essay from the students; they will, furthermore, be justified in criticizing it if the student hasn't addressed himself to the problem, or has merely copied out other people's opinions, or has written unintelligibly; or if he is unwilling to discuss what he has written. Once a teacher has explained to his pupil what the point of the writing and criticizing of essays is, then his own attitude to this pupil's essays must become serious, to live up to the now explicit expectations of the pupil. Thus, not only would students' grasp of what they are supposed to be doing be improved, but so would the teachers' peformance of their own role.

Furthermore, to see clearly what kinds of problems your subject is supposed to have before it may well be made clearer to a student by contrast with the kinds of problems peculiar to other subjects. Thus a grasp, not of the superficial aspects of a lot of different subjects, but of the conceptual relation between different subjects may well be the outcome. Thus the student, at the end of his period of higher education, might well find himself able to understand, not a little bit about other subjects, but rather what other subjects are like and what would count as a serious and fruitful way of pursuing them, if he had time or inclination or money to do so. Self-consciousness about what he himself is up to goes along with awareness of what other people are up to, in different disciplines. This I suspect is the aspect of higher education which no one would wish to see sacrificed.

ACADEMIC FREEDOM

Should there be a monolithic or a binary system of higher education in this country? Should there be clear guide-lines on the curriculum laid down by a central body? Should teachers in higher education be trained? Should there be a central organization to ensure their continuing education and the development of their professional skills? Should institutions be forced to adapt to the needs of adult as well as young students? Should there be a division among staff between those who teach first-year students and those who teach the rest, with varying expectations of research from each? Should teachers in higher education have tenure? Should there be merit awards? To raise all these questions may be educative and in that sense valuable. But the answer to all of them may in the end be the same. Whatever would or would not be desirable, one cannot legislate. For this would be to infringe, and ultimately to erode, academic freedom. Lurking behind all the questions and answers we have considered is the other great question, is academic freedom the highest value? Is it that which must override all other considerations? For if it is, then we may wish and long for things to be different, but we cannot plan that they should be. One can deliberate, Aristotle said, only about the possible. And to act in breach of academic freedom is not possible. Freedom constitutes a categorical imperative against which no considerations of what is expedient or even what is desirable have any weight.

In this third part of my chapter I shall briefly look at such claims. For this is the tone in which academic freedom is often mentioned. But do we really believe in it so passionately? It is certain that, if we did, then none of the propositions put forward in these papers would be of more than purely theoretical or hypothetical interest. Though anyone would be free to try to set up an independent new institution of higher education incorporating the suggestions here made, there would be no conceivable way, apart from the power of example, to make other institutions change to come in line.

We might perhaps profitably pursue a bit further what it is that we mean by academic freedom. Freedom is, like other rights, a concept that makes sense only if it is understood as something claimed against a particular background. More precisely, freedom becomes a value only in contrast with a specific threat. Nor do we need to seek very far for the threat against which we demand academic freedom. It is the political threat, that education shall be made to serve the ends of a particular government. We have examples, both historical and contemporary, to make us fear this beyond everything. We profoundly believe that we are entitled to think what we like, and discover what we can. This is what constitutes the love of academic freedom. It is this that above all we wish to defend. And, ideally, the possession of such freedom entails that we should be able to teach what we like to whom so ever we choose, using what methods we prefer. For if the pursuit of truth is what we value most highly in research (truth, even if it is disagreeable politically or disruptive socially), if the aim of teaching is not so much to hand on received dogma, as to enable students themselves to pursue truth wherever they see it, then we should be prepared to defend whatever we believe to be the best means to achieve these desirable ends. Seen in this context, control over the structures and methods of universities, no less than the control over curriculum content, can be interpreted as authoritarian, an infringement of academic freedom. To insist, for example, that only qualified teachers should hold university posts, or that all students should take courses of a particular kind in their first year, such things could become weapons for muzzling the innovatory, excluding the eccentric, stifling experiment. We should be able to establish new institutions of education and research if there are none in existence which come up to our standards. But of course this ideal cannot be fully realized because of finance. We fully understand that if institutions of higher education were, like independent schools, totally self-supporting, then only the rich would be able to benefit from them, and that offends another ideal, that of equality, or at least mobility within society. We accept therefore, that universities and polytechnics will be paid for out of public funds, one way or another.

It is at this stage, of course, that the argument of social justice and democracy demands that we should listen to the voices which, as we have seen, say that institutions of higher education should be *accountable to society*. This is a version of the reasonable belief that he who pays the piper calls the tune. In order to restrain the piper's paymaster, and keep his demands within bounds, we adopt two strategies. One is to pretend that there is a line to be drawn between the social demands of society and the political demands of government. I believe that such a distinction is in fact impossible to draw. If it looks plausible, it is only because fortunately we still have a certain measure of agreement, shared by all governments and by most educationalists, about what provision there should be. The requirement that institutions should be 'accountable' is a political demand; but it is disguised because on the whole, and very broadly, political parties are satisfied with the products of higher education. But we are now, in the 1980s, in a position where for the first time we can see what it would be like if this broad consensus on the utility of the universities disappeared.

The second strategy we adopt is one which has had, I believe, enormous success in this country, and should not be underestimated. That is the 'arm's-length' strategy. We fully acknowledge that public money pays for institutions of higher education but we place a buffer between them and the ultimate paymaster, which has a degree of autonomy, and a range of freedom of choice in the allocation of funds. The local authorities are used as a rather inefficient buffer in the case of the polytechnics, the UGC in the case of the universities. Thus though there is not complete freedom, there is the *illusion of freedom*, because there are actual choices to be made. And perhaps this is all that freedom can ever amount to. However, successful though the arm's-length principle is, whether applied to education or to broadcasting, it is open to attack on two grounds. First, it can be directly attacked as being a fraud on the public. Despite protestations to the contrary, it is alleged that there is direct pressure from government on the buffer organizations, either through the political nature of the appointments to it (consider the row about Hoggart leaving the Arts Council — even though his term of office was up), or through various threats to withdraw funds, unless a political line is toed. Secondly, it can be attacked on the ground that such a system itself perpetuates a kind of conservatism within the institutions that are funded. There is no place for experiment or innovation, if a collection of relatively ignorant non-specialist amateurs is in charge of distributing funds. Only truly self-funded institutions could afford to be other than, at best, slow to change, at worst ossified.

These then are the criticisms of the arm's-length principle. But it may be the best we can do. There are no new or profound insights here. Nor, I think, is there any single best possible solution (and this may itself constitute a kind of argument for diversity, including the retention of the binary system). When we express in our arguments a sincerely held value-judgement in favour of academic freedom, it is as well to remember that we have also claimed to value public accountability, and that these values may conflict. To repeat, if we see that all institutions of higher education would be improved if their aims were clearly and rationally stated; if the areas of overlap between their functions were ironed out; if teachers in all of these were paid and graded on a single system; if they could be encouraged to improve their teaching techniques and professional skills; if they could be sacked for incompetence — if we see all this and want it badly enough, then we should be bold enough to lobby for the view that such useful improvements do not constitute a threat, or at least not the kind of political threat the fear of which prompts us to assert our right of freedom. We must attempt to draw a philosophical distinction between social dictatorship and political dictatorship. If such a line could be drawn, we might be able to argue that control over the finance, structure and teaching methods, even over the taught curriculum of institutions of higher education is simply a matter of social accountability. It is nothing more, we could say, than an expression of openness and sensitivity to the needs and the mood of society. And if we are trusting, we can say that society prefers the truth to be pursued, and therefore the central, and crucial, freedom to pursue it cannot be threatened by controls of this kind. Political control would be something different. It would demand that certain courses should not be taught, that certain research should not be undertaken or published. Only that kind of control would count as a threat to freedom. Personally, as I have suggested, I do not feel confident that such a line can be drawn with any theoretical or philosophical justification. On the other hand I am sure that we have to try to draw it for practical reasons. And if we do, we might be ready to keep careful watch in case one kind of control begins to spill over into the other.

Perhaps the most important point is the final one.

Within any sphere whatever, in the arts, in morals and, above all, in politics, there is the risk that we shall value things that are incompatible. And I do not mean that within any society people will disagree with each other about values, though that is true. It is rather that each individual values numbers of things which may conflict. Thus an individual teacher in higher education may well value both freedom to pursue the truth (and to publish what he finds) and the social responsibility of the institution where he works. All we can hope for is that nothing we really rate high is utterly neglected, no purpose we seriously want to pursue totally frustrated. To ensure this somewhat modest good, we must, as we all know, be prepared for compromise and constant vigilance.

REFERENCE
Boyle, E. and Crosland, A. (1971) *The Politics of Education* Maurice Kogan

4

FREEDOMS, RIGHTS AND ACCOUNTABILITY

by Donald Bligh

This final chapter of the second of the two volumes devoted to the SRHE Leverhulme seminar on the teaching function, does not present the conclusions of the seminar. Its conclusions form the recommendations given in the first chapter of the first volume, *Professionalism and Flexibility for Learning*.

This chapter is devoted to three general issues related to staffing, which arose during the seminar but which did not receive very thorough treatment and which need to be resolved by the higher education community. They are all associated with gradual trends in the relationships of staff:

1 With the government and public opinion.
2 With their students.
3 With their departments and institutions.

WHAT ACADEMIC FREEDOMS IN TEACHING CAN BE JUSTIFIED?

The cluster of questions that seems to underpin all staff relationships is concerned with academic freedoms and responsibilities. The first chapter of *Professionalism and Flexibility for Learning* recommends that matters to do with teaching should be more open than at present and should be subject to regular peer reviews. It was proposed that courses should be more student-centred and more flexible in their arrangements. In particular, institutions should place more emphasis upon the needs of older students. The recommendations in that chapter advocate developing departmental specialists in course design and course management, and developing ways to increase the mobility of staff. As Mary Warnock points out in Chapter 3 of this volume, to make such recommendations will be perceived by many academic staff as a threat to their academic freedom.

Yet it is not obvious what freedoms in teaching are being claimed or how such claims are justified. Everyone seems to agree that academic freedom should be defended, but there is little agreement or clarity about what it is. Unless we know what it is and can justify it, we will neither defend it convincingly nor exercise it responsibly in the coming decade.

Hence, in spite of its acclaim, it is in the defence of academic freedom that we need a new consensus. It was not threatened very much in the years of expansion and our vigilance has slackened. Now a contracting system of higher education, a less favourable public image, a widespread growth in unemployment and a harsher political scene are not conducive to seemingly privileged freedoms.

Indeed when arguments for academic freedoms are analysed they give some support for freedoms based upon general civil liberties, but the claims for special privileges as teachers look weak.

What are the arguments? Many have been given (see for example Pincoffs 1972) and no doubt some readers will protest if I do not give their preferred argument. One of the most influential accounts of academic freedom in recent years has been by Searle (1972) who distinguishes two complementary theories.

Theory

On one view academic freedom is a particular group of some general civil liberties (cf Searle 1972). Any citizen in our society is free to seek the truth about anything he likes, and to pass it on to others, except where the freedom is explicitly taken away. For example, in the case of military secrets, recent Cabinet papers, one company's chemical formulae, another company's production processes, and many other areas of knowledge, the freedom to inquire and expound is taken away. It is also surrendered during working hours when most people take a job, because it is implicit in the terms of accepting the job that the employee will spend his working time on the firm's business, not on something else. But in the case of higher education the firm's business *is* that its members should seek new knowledge by critical inquiry (a research function) and pass it on to others as they see it (a teaching function). It would therefore be contrary to the implicit contract between employer and employee to sack him, or in some other way penalize him, for doing what he was asked to do. Such freedoms are not unique to teachers in higher education. The man in the street may enjoy them in his own time.

Within this limited statement of the General Theory of academic freedom there are, of course, many assumptions. I shall pick on four.

Functions and Contracts First, the particular application of this general principle of civil liberty depends upon the function of institutions of higher education, part of which is pursued in the role of the academic. It also assumes that there is an implicit contract between the academic and his institution which allows the academic certain freedoms.

Free Critical Inquiry Secondly, there is a set of assumptions about how knowledge is obtained. Since the time of Descartes, the accepted methods for obtaining knowledge have not been to refer to the dogma of presupposed authorities, but have included independent observation, the principle of public verification, the dissemination and testing of opinions, and the contesting of them. This process of critical inquiry, in which no belief is immune from doubt, has become fundamental to the pursuit of knowledge in higher education.

Civil Liberties Thirdly, it is assumed that whatever the exceptions, we live in a society in which certain civil liberties exist as the norm: namely the rights to discover and disseminate the truth unhindered.

The Value of Knowledge Fourthly, in that kind of society it is easier than in some others to value the truth, not only as sometimes useful, but as having some intrinsic and possibly absolute value. (Mary Warnock's position on page 114 seems close to this.) For example, academics may claim to study a subject 'for its own sake', not for its beneficial consequences (cf Leavis 1972). If so, their values may be called 'non-consequentialist'. There is a freedom to research into, and to teach, subjects that are not obviously useful.

The Special Theory
On the Special Theory the academic claims a special authority and privilege not possessed by the general population as a civil right. It is therefore applicable in countries that do not have the same general civil liberties as Britain does. Even in this country there are government regulations controlling the selection and rejection of the disabled and other minority groups for employment, the contents of packaged food, the statements made in advertisements, and the certification of building standards; but in the pursuit of their profession within their institutions academic staff claim freedom from outside interference. For example lecturers claim the right

— To select and reject their students.
— To devise the content of their own curricula.
— To oblige students to consider their opinions.
— To validate and issue certificates on the competence of others.

Universities, polytechnics and colleges of higher education are publicly supported institutions but claim immunity from public control and interference.

A Consequentialist Value of Knowledge In a society without civil liberties we take for granted, academic freedom would have to be given as a special privilege. Hence it would probably, though not necessarily, be given because the knowledge consequent upon such freedom is seen to be useful. Thus there is an assumption about the value of academic freedom based upon its consequences (ie a consequentialist value). There is no assumption that searching for the truth has some absolute value that should never be compromised. It is simply that knowing the truth is often useful.

The Special Competence of Academics and their Institutions The crux of the Special Theory is (a) a claim that academics have a special competence or expertise in the search for truth and (b) a claim that they possess special knowledge of their subject. This distinction is important. To deny (a) is to suppress the truth. To deny (b) is to challenge the intellectual authority of academics. (a) and (b) overlap in that if academics carry out research they can claim knowledge that others do not have, because they have explored and tested ideas in fields unvisited by others.

Variants of the first two assumptions of the General Theory can be used when pleading for academic freedom as a special privilege; namely, the special function of academics and the use of free critical inquiry.

The Special Function of Academics Institutions of higher education are specially concerned with seeking and disseminating the truth. However, there is also a special claim that the academic's contract is different from most contracts with employers. It is not necessarily a contract to do with what the employer wants. The contract is not, and cannot be, to prejudge, find and proclaim particular assertions as true, but to seek, find and proclaim *the* truth. Thus an academic should not be penalized for finding and publishing unpopular truths.

The Use of Free Critical Inquiry Discovering the truth needs a process of doubt (or at least, suspended belief) and free inquiry.

I am not pretending that this is a full account of the argument for academic freedom. There is, in any case, no generally accepted argument. The philosophy on this subject is remarkably tangled. My account is different from John Searle's (1972), but it is strongly influenced by it. The account is obviously a sketch of a selected number of points without cautious qualification or reservation.

Both the General and Special arguments could be applicable in Britain. They each cover some cases not covered by the other. They are complementary and not in conflict. The General Theory covers several freedoms not covered by the Special Theory, for example the freedom of the press. I am not concerned to discuss the detailed formulation of these freedoms as philosophy. My intention is first to use the sketch as a springboard to raise a number of points that will need to be clarified in the next few years if the concept of academic freedom is not to be discredited, and secondly to show that academic freedom does not include freedoms in teaching commonly attributed to it.

What Freedoms in Teaching are being Claimed?
So far as teaching is concerned there needs to be much greater clarity about what freedoms are being claimed. What seems to emerge is that academic freedom is a collective name for a number of separate freedoms such as:

A Freedom of inquiry — freedom to pursue the truth unhindered, and by methods including doubt, criticism, discussion and testing of any belief.
B Freedom to disseminate the truth as one sees it.
C Freedom to express doubts and criticisms of any belief.
D Freedom to decide who shall be members of one's own academic institution(s).
E Freedom to decide the content of academic courses.
F Freedom to decide upon the competence and certification of others.

Freedom to do each of these things is taken to mean that academics who do them will be free from threats, particularly threats of dismissal. Freedoms A to C may be justified both on the ground that they are each a general civil liberty (General Theory) and that academics have a special competence in the search for truth (Special Theory). But it seems to me that Freedoms D to F are not based upon the need for free critical inquiry, but upon a claim by academics to have authority because they know more than other people about their subject. They depend upon claim (b) of the Special Theory.

Claims for tenure, syllabus control and the privacy of teaching are not obviously justified by the theories of academic freedom. While it may not be possible to separate the research and teaching roles of academics, Freedom A is particularly concerned with research; Freedoms E and F are mostly concerned with teaching; and Freedoms B to D are clearly related to both.

The theories say little directly about freedoms in teaching. They support some freedom for the expression of opinions when teaching, but they provide better arguments for preserving the Social Science Research Council than for preserving the tenure of teachers. Yet academic staff often wish to make claims for academic freedom in matters to do with tenure that have nothing to do with freedom from threats of dismissal for expressing unpopular opinions. Similarly some academics have believed that they are protected from redundancy on the grounds of their academic freedom; yet it is difficult to see that issues of academic freedom are in the least way relevant. Staff may be protected on the basis of tenure agreements within their contracts of employment; but that is another matter. It is hard to see any reason why academic freedom should justify, still less necessitate, such agreements. According to the General Theory academic freedom is dependent upon the nature of the contract, not the other way round.

Academic freedom in teaching often amounts to claims to teach what one likes how one likes. These claims need to be justified, but the General Theory and claim (a) of the Special Theory will not do. It does not follow that, because academics should be free to disseminate the truth as they see it in subjects of their choice, they should not be compelled to teach the truth as they see it in subjects not of their choosing. Freedom B implies freedom from disseminating ideas one believes to be false, and Freedoms B and C imply freedom to express one's belief that certain truths are unimportant; but however much these freedoms justify the inclusion of X in the syllabus, additional arguments are required to justify the exclusion of Y. Admittedly, additional arguments may not be hard to find, because if staff are free to teach X it is not difficult to claim that staff, time or other resources are insufficient to teach Y. The important point, however, is that academic freedom is not necessary to, but contingent upon these circumstances. It leaves the onus upon staff in each case to show what the circumstances are and to show that the principles of academic freedom apply.

The freedom to teach what one likes how one likes is based upon a claim to authority in matters of teaching (ie claim (b) of the Special Theory) but this, we shall see, is shaky, at least in some cases.

In practice the General Theory may be no stronger on matters of curriculum control. Whatever high ideals the non-consequentialist such as F.R. Leavis may hold, the simple political fact is that governments have to consider consequences. The days are numbered in which, as the government may see it, a self-selected élite may continue studying subjects for their own sakes at the nation's expense. Non-consequentialist ethics are in disfavour. The nation looks for economic justifications for educational expenditure. Some subjects seem more likely to bring national economic benefit than others. Is it not the government's duty to cultivate the study of these subjects? (Mary Warnock (pages 101 ff.) alludes to this in reminding us of Crosland's thoughts in establishing the polytechnics. Blume (1982) makes a similar point with reference to research.)

Again, attempts to preserve the privacy of teaching have sometimes been justified on the ground of academic freedom; while one might have thought that the moral obligation to disseminate the truth might lead to the opposite conclusion!

None of this precludes the possibility that good arguments can be found to preserve the tenure, syllabus control and privacy of teachers. It is simply to say that traditional arguments for academic freedom are insufficient justification.

Comparison with Schoolteachers
Any argument for freedoms in matters of teaching will need to take account of how far the same freedoms should be offered to schoolteachers. I am not saying that academic freedom should, or should not, be claimed by schoolteachers (although many would rarely claim it for themselves), only that the consequences of any argument need to be worked out in the context of schools as well as higher education. For example, it is common to claim academic freedom to control what is taught within a discipline on the basis of the academic's expertise in his subject; schoolteachers too have an expertise in their subject at the level at which they

teach it, yet their freedom of choice is often marginal. The academics' case on the ground of special competence would be stronger if academics could claim that they are teaching so near the frontiers of knowledge that they, and only they, have knowledge of the subject matter to be taught. Schoolteachers cannot make this claim; but, manifestly, neither can many academic staff, particularly in subjects like chemistry where the frontiers of knowledge are far beyond undergraduate level, or subjects like psychology, philosophy, accountancy and medicine which most students study as a new subject and must therefore begin at an elementary level.

When is Special Competence Relevant?
Thus the argument on the basis of special competence begins to look shaky when it is analysed in detail. This point can be illustrated in other ways. An important area of academic freedom is the right of institutions to choose what courses they should provide. It may be possible to justify this freedom on general grounds of institutional autonomy; but in specific cases the argument can be weak if argued on the basis of academic freedom of the individual. For example, if the case for accepting or rejecting a particular course is made on a consequentialist basis to do with the employability of its graduates, it is by no means obvious that academics will be the people most competent to decide who will be most employable. Similarly, if the government were to instruct an institution to set up a department of occupational therapy instead of the department of computer science which it wanted, objections by the institution, on the ground of the special freedom derived from its academic competence, are likely to be weak if, at that stage, the institution has specialists in neither discipline.

Another difficulty lies in defining the area of special competence. The area is quite different according to the argument used to justify academic freedom. *Using claim (a)*, the area of special competence to teach has a more restricted boundary than one's area for research. A researcher may reasonably claim special competence to explore the unknown and in the process of research the boundary for exploration may be very wide, if indeed there could be a boundary at all. Research includes looking for hitherto unimagined connections in subjects previously thought to be distant. Teaching is less exploratory. It is much more concerned with expounding what is known than exploring what is unknown. There would be something odd about claiming special competence and freedoms to teach the unknown, in a way that is not true of research.

But what, then, is the area of special competence over which teachers, rather than researchers, can claim freedoms? An academic cannot claim to be an expert in every subject using claim (b). Is his special competence in teaching confined to his subject and if so, is its boundary defined by his academic department? The area of expertise would probably be even more restricted if it was to be justified *using claim* (*b*) on the basis of knowledge acquired through his own research. But in practice we often have to teach aspects of our subject quite remote from our research interests. At the SRHE Leverhulme seminar we heard that E, the freedom to choose what academics teach, is being challenged (eg by professional organizations and local education authorities). If academics wish to retain this freedom they may need to be clearer about its justification and limits than they have been in the past.

Many of the recommendations made in *Professionalism and Flexibility for Learning* are concerned with how academics teach. It would be unconvincing to object to these recommendations on the grounds of the universal special competence of academics in techniques of teaching. Academics have considerably less formal training in teaching than almost any other sector of the teaching professions (see Chapter 2, pp. 57 ff.).

Teaching Criticism of the Establishment
A better argument, and one that can most easily exclude the comparison with schoolteachers, is that the post-Cartesian process of free critical inquiry is not appropriate in schools, but that it is the definitive characteristic of teaching in higher education. (Some teachers of Nuffield Science and CSE Mode 3 courses in schools would not agree.) This argument also has the advantage that it is drawn so that there is no relation to research activities. It may therefore apply to institutions of higher education where little research is done.

The obvious objection to the argument is that most teaching in higher education will not pass the proposed test — critical inquiry. Simple observation will show that most teaching, even in universities where most research is done, is not of the kind claimed. In the teaching of some subjects, most of all in the sciences and engineering (which paradoxically have benefited greatly from the Cartesian legacy), the process of learning by doubt and critical inquiry is crowded out by getting across the 'established truths'. Yet one might think that a claim for academic freedom in teaching on the grounds of pursuing the truth where ever the pursuit may lead, can only be justified if the teaching styles manifest free critical inquiry. The point could be expressed more strongly: if we have an obligation (as distinct from a freedom) to pursue the truth, this principle should inform our teaching. It should allow the expression of varied views, the testing of beliefs, the weighing of evidence and the exercise of reason; but observation suggests that the dominant styles of teaching in higher education do not encourage doubt.

Teachers in higher education could reply that while the cultivation of doubt and criticism is the hallmark of a higher education, that does not mean that higher education should consist of nothing else. Much time must be taken in laying the foundations upon which the ability to criticize is based.

However, the views expressed in the last two paragraphs are not in conflict. It is consistent with both views to conclude that freedom to teach students to seek the truth by constant doubt, criticism and testing of established beliefs is an important academic freedom in teaching, and to conclude that, at present, teachers in higher education do not live up to the standards of free critical inquiry in their teaching. The apparent conflict arises from a mismatch between our academic ideals and our teaching in practice.

Justification by Evaluation?
Practical teaching is not the only aspect of an academic's work that is open to observation and test. In principle any area in which academics claim special competence is open to scrutiny. The claim to possess special competence is itself not immune from doubt and critical inquiry. In this way, far from being a threat to academic freedom, a constant evaluation and re-evaluation of an academic's research and teaching provides opportunities for constant vindication of competence — and hence the constant vindication of academic freedoms based upon the Special Theory.

This point is important. Academic freedom, like many other freedoms, needs to be continually defended. In the long run it is not defended by the use of power, but by favourable public opinion arising from the evident responsibility with which the freedom is used. The price of academic freedom is vigilance — not against threats from others, but against a deterioration of our own standards. Academic freedom is not a right, but a privilege that is earned.

However, much depends upon the form of the evaluation of competence and responsibility. In the Special Theory the evaluation of competence and responsibility is associated with the evaluation of the consequences of academic freedom. Such consequences would, and should, take years to discern. Sufficient time is necessary to make a sound generalization. The idea that academic freedom could be a special privilege which governments, or others, could withdraw if the consequence of such freedom were not *generally* beneficial, may seem like no freedom at all, if an academic's work is constantly disturbed by necessity for short-term instrumentalism, by an anxiety always to be 'beneficial', or by a vigilance not to offend the government.

The balance of these interests lies in the word 'generally'. If, before any valid generalization can be made, a government is swift to clamp down on any teaching of which it disapproves, there will be little sense of academic freedom. But if academics were to abuse their freedom, for example so as to narrow medical curricula dangerously, their freedom becomes academic licence.

Who should arbitrate in such cases? Constraints upon the abuse of academic freedom might be exercised by the government, the academics themselves, or an independent body such as the CNAA, the UGC or an ombudsman. Since such independent bodies are dominated by academics (although this could change) they offer a form of peer review. Thus the use of regular peer reviews, as recommended in *Professionalism and Flexibility for Learning*, is a way to preserve academic freedoms in an increasingly consequentialist world, rather than a threat to diminish them.

How else can governments acknowledge the value of academic freedoms in teaching? In the long run the most effective safeguard to maintain academic freedom is not the argument of the General and Special Theories, but the provision of such excellent teaching that when today's students reach positions of influence, both they, and those they influence, will be grateful for the quality of education they received.

A CONTRACT BETWEEN STUDENT AND INSTITUTION?

For some readers the idea of an educational contract will seem so repugnant that they will react angrily and will not wish to consider it; but, like the implications of the falling birthrate, it will not go away by being ignored. Black and Sparkes (1982) have shown that it is time to take a long hard look at the style of relationships between teachers and students in higher education. Relationships between students have changed a great deal since before the swinging 60s and with the expansion of our institutions, but the conventions of teaching have changed less.

Indeed several of the recommendations given in *Professionalism and Flexibility for Learning* imply the need for a new kind of relationship between teachers and their students. They seem to imply a greater esteem for students than in the past. For example it is recommended that courses should be manifestly 'student-centred', that there should be flexible patterns of, and access to, courses for individuals in higher education, that more emphasis should be placed upon the needs of older students, that students could be assessed without having taken a specific route to prepare for the assessment, and that teachers should help students take maximum responsibility for their own learning. These things seem to show a greater respect for students and to expect more maturity from them than has previously been common. They are out of keeping with the view that what students want is unimportant and they should do as they are told.

Staff/student relationships are likely to change, not because virtually all students now *legally* have adult status, but because of a growing recognition that a significant proportion of students are indeed adults, with experience to bring to their learning not possessed by their teachers; that students *morally* have rights, duties and responsibilities; that the authoritarian and paternalistic norms of the past are now inappropriate; that the style of relationships common in the education of schoolchildren has been inappropriately transferred to teaching in higher education; that, as in industry, people only work their best with consultation and explanation about what is required; and that institutions of higher education provide a service to, and are financially dependent upon, their clients, the students.

Respect for students is not something upon which one can legislate or pronounce national policies, but, if there is a changing relationship, in the long run the form of 'contract' between students and their educational institutions will need to reflect the change. No doubt many aspects of the relationships between students and their institutions are not contractual at all, but are governed by the charter, statutes, ordinances, and so on of the institution.

It might be argued that there is not, and should not be any formal or legal contract; that such a thing is in the interests of neither students nor their teachers; that the relationships we value most in higher education would be damaged if they were formalized; that contracts encourage people to do the minimum to satisfy them; that striving for excellence goes beyond any obligations a contract could reasonably require; and that the academic freedom of both staff and students is best preserved by the absence of legal entanglements. Furthermore, many complaints that students might wish to bring would not be within the jurisdiction of the courts.

However, on several occasions the courts have recognized that there is a contract, and, whether we like it or not, the greater the tensions in higher education and the greater the financial and personal investment in it, the more cases will inevitably be brought. Consequently, case law will gradually accumulate, almost without our knowing. There are other areas of life in which the law has steadily encroached upon personal relationships. I neither applaud nor denounce this tendency. For the moment I only want to recognize that it exists.

If so, there will be a need to work out what the relationship should be. Consequently the nature and extent of the contract between a student and his institution is an issue that thinking people in higher education should ponder. It is not an issue to decide in a hurry or at a seminar. It requires consensus. In the past one might have expected that the contract would be a contract of licence for consideration (I extend the use of the term somewhat), but with a rise in the status of students it could be a negotiated contract.

A Contract of Licence for Consideration
Under a contract of licence for consideration a student applies to a college for permission to use its facilities: for instance to attend its lectures, to use its laboratories and library, to enjoy its atmosphere, and so on. No doubt the medieval university was of this kind. Young students sought permission to join a community of older scholars.

On this view of higher education, a student is entitled to be a very junior member of the academic club provided he abides by the rules; but he has no say in what the rules are (probably some are enshrined in the institutions' constitution), he cannot change the menu of courses, he probably has to accept the dish he is offered and he may not be allowed to reject any part of it. For this privilege he pays fees or sums are paid on his behalf. There is no guarantee of the quality of teaching from the institution. Furthermore the nature of the rules and regulations is not always clear. The student must get himself informed from a variety of sources, such as the prospectus, the university calendar, semi-official documents, and even spoken advice. The contract is not a single document.

A contract of licence for consideration is one-sided. Consider, for example, the content of a course. Since it is impossible to teach every part of a subject it will necessarily be selective. The selection is not a matter of negotiation; it is made by the academic staff either on the basis of their superior knowledge or in response to their personal preferences. It may be said that if the selection is made before any student accepts a place, no student should complain about the content of a course. Acceptance of a place is acceptance of a contract for a course as specified. But in practice it is not possible to specify the objectives or content of a course in such detail that no dispute could ever arise. Course specifications are inevitably imprecise. In any case complete specification is hardly desirable. Subjects develop rapidly. If graduates are to emerge with up-to-date knowledge, the curriculum contract must be changeable. At whose discretion should it be changed? Surely the academic staff are the only people with sufficient up-to-date knowledge to decide. If the contract is a licence for consideration it will be emphasized, particularly when students first apply to college and when they seek to undertake a discipline they have not studied before, that they have insufficient knowledge of their subject to discuss, let alone negotiate, their own curriculum. With scattered documentation and no negotiation, students don't always understand what they are letting themselves in for. For the students, but not for the teachers, a course of study is a journey into the unknown. Furthermore they cannot easily withdraw from it, or transfer to another course, without loss of face, time, grants and credibility. For the students much is at stake; for the staff there is little risk. The staff have control and relative security of tenure. Thus it is a contract in which staff can be selective, imprecise, and change the terms, while for students it is a contract to which they are heavily committed, which they do not understand and over which they have almost no control. Nevertheless the rewards for students are high — a degree — and thousands apply every year.

I do not know whether this form of contract is the most appropriate. I am more concerned that others should judge it than that I should do so. I have presented a rather stark view of it so that the reader may at least question what many have tacitly taken for granted, because in the next few years the form of the contract, if any, between students and their institutions may need to be reconsidered, clarified and set out in a single document.

A Negotiated Contract
The obvious alternative to a contract of licence for consideration is a

negotiated contract. The extent of matters for negotiation would be determined by the constitution of the institution.

In a negotiated contract students promise to study and thereby to learn, and the teachers promise to teach. This is not, of course, to say that students promise to learn everything the teachers try to teach them, nor that teachers should try to teach everything the students ought or want to learn. It does mean that both teachers and students have rights and obligations with respect to each other. Students are customers or clients and fees are paid in return for goods and services supplied by the teachers. The content, method and style of a course should bear some resemblance to that which teachers promised to supply.

Some of the rights bestowed by a negotiated contract are uncontentious. For example most people would agree that examiners should undertake to assess and to grade students fairly and only on the basis of their academic merit.

On a negotiated contract students have a right, if not a duty, to seek the truth. If, in order to justify academic freedom in teaching, academics claim that teaching is a process of free critical inquiry, students must be engaged in the same process and should therefore enjoy corresponding freedoms. Students may have an obligation to learn the subjects on the courses they agreed to take, but they also have a right to learn about other subjects than those that they were accepted by an institution to study. This means that because discussion, the sharing of ideas, the weighing of evidence and the exercise of reason are part of the post-Cartesian method by which students learn, students have a right to be heard and a right to hear others (although no one has an obligation to speak or to listen).

It is often part of the students' contracts that they will be offered a certificate or formal award if their academic performance is of a certain (usually unspecified) standard. Perhaps students' rights to do with assessment are less negotiable than many others. Nonetheless the certificate has some legal status and students' rights that pertain to it should be clearly documented when students enter college.

There are enormous difficulties in the conception of a negotiated contract between students and their academic institution. Nonetheless they are difficulties that must be overcome if relationships between staff and students are to be valued by both (see Recommendation 1.2d in Chapter 1 in *Professionalism and Flexibility for Learning*). First, it would be impractical to negotiate a separate contract with every student. Most clauses would need to be standard. This would undermine the individual approach implied by a negotiated contract.

Secondly, in every part of the contract there are implicit standards and value judgements which are very difficult to define, to judge, to maintain and even more difficult to enforce. For example, there is an implicit promise to teach effectively, but what are the criteria of effective teaching and what standard of teaching would a court of law hold it reasonable to expect?

Thirdly, teachers must be allowed some latitude to vary their courses from what they have advertised, if only to keep them up-to-date, but what variation is reasonable? If an institution offered a unique course because they employed a professor who had knowledge not possessed by anyone else, and if the professor suddenly died, it would not seem reasonable for students to sue their college for breach of contract in failing to supply the course for which they were accepted. (Presumably the institution could ensure that there was some kind of disclaimer clause.)

Fourthly, there is a sense in which one man's freedom is another man's constraint — will a respect for students' rights curtail academic freedoms? For example the National Union of Students and the National Council for Civil Liberties (1970) foresaw that students might wish to criticize the teaching of a member of staff with regard to

i   The clarity and coherence of his exposition.
ii   The relevance of what he teaches to the published syllabus.
iii   His factual accuracy.
iv   His interpretation of his subject.

They saw the first three as legitimate and the fourth as only a threat to academic freedom if it was discussed *within* the governmental processes of the institution.

Such questions of criticism and constraint raise a third major issue.

HOW AND TO WHOM ARE TEACHERS ACCOUNTABLE?

The demand for professionalism and flexibility from teachers assumes that they should be accountable (see Chapter 3, page 107), but for what are they accountable, how, and to whom? No doubt for individuals it depends upon who you are. For institutions in higher education there has long been a principle that they should not be directly accountable to central government; yet in the long run institutions must be accountable to those who provide their finance, but how long should 'the long run' be?

If teaching institutions must be accountable, inevitably the accountability must be passed down to the individuals who do the teaching. But how far do the claims for the autonomy of institutions and the academic freedom of individuals conflict with demands for accountability? A resolution of this conflict, if it is a conflict, is one of the problems that must be faced by higher education in the coming decade. A prerequisite to its resolution is a clear understanding of the different kinds of accountability.

Individuals and institutions could be held to be accountable in either sense of 'accountability' mentioned by Mary Warnock in Chapter 3. They may give an account of what they have done, perhaps in terms of what its consequences have been, or they may seek the acquiescence, sanction or support of the government or some other organization to whom they are responsible and which thereby exercises influence and even control. In the first sense, an institution gives an account of itself in the announcement of its degree awards. Institutions of higher education would be accountable in the second sense if they had to obtain the permission of (local) government or other bodies to put on courses of their choosing, or if (local) government could oblige institutions to provide any courses it chose.

Most people would agree that the first kind of accountability is compatible with academic freedom; in the past it has generally been accepted that the second is not. The role of government or other organizations in the first case is to receive information and the role of the higher education institution is to provide it. In the second case both these roles persist, but the government is also exercising initiative, control and power in matters normally regarded as requiring academic discretion.

Thus far my view is the same as Mary Warnock's, but it can be taken a little further. It seems to me that although the distinction between these two kinds of accountability is very sharp, there are, in practice, a large number of intermediate levels of freedom and accountability which are much less clear. It is the very presence and fuzziness of the intermediate distinctions that makes precedents for the infringement of academic freedom so easy to establish. In practice there is a slippery transition from academic freedom to academic servitude, from 'giving an account' to 'being accountable'. If there are going to be increasing pressures upon academic freedom in the next ten to fifteen years, and if academics are to resist these pressures, they will need to be vigilant. The vigilance will require a very clear conception of the line that must not be transgressed. If the pressures upon individuals are going to increase (whether or not they increase upon institutions) the rank and file of academics will need a clearer perception of the many intermediate positions than they have had in the past.

Giving a Voluntary Account
A university, polytechnic or college may enjoy maximum freedom and minimal accountability if it voluntarily gives an account of what it has done to the University Grants Committee (UGC), a local education authority (LEA), the National Advisory Body (NAB), the Council for National Academic Awards (CNAA), a professional body, the Department of Education and Science (DES), or some other external agent. Similarly, a teacher may report what he has taught or how he has taught it to his head of department, faculty board or other colleagues in positions of power. The colleagues or external agent would infringe academic freedom least if they received the report without making adverse comments. Indeed the authors of the report would *feel* the greatest freedom if it was received with encouragement.

The essence of accountability in this case is the provision and receipt of information. The information could be a description, an explanation or a justification. Decisions and actions that have to be justified are less free than those that are only described, because they are confined by the limits of reason.

Being Obliged to Report Formally
The freedom of an institution or an individual is diminished if they are *obliged* to give an account. The origin of such obligations may be diverse. They may, for example, be self-imposed moral obligations, customs set by precedent, or statutory requirements. Whatever the origin or sanction, although there is considerable freedom to decide what the account, or report, shall contain, there is little freedom to withhold it.

Being Answerable
Freedom to decide the content of a report will be curtailed if the UGC, LEA, DES, head of department, or whoever the external agent may be, seeks further clarification of what the institution or individual has done. The clarification may require a description, explanation or justification. At this stage the external agent is no longer a passive recipient of a report. It is minimally responsive and it seeks specific information.

In so far as any institution is open to official inspection, must annually give an account of its financial affairs, or must supply certain information to auditors and tax inspectors, the principle behind this kind of accountability is well-established. Nor should these examples lead the reader to think that it is only central government that requires such accounts to be given. For example the UGC has long prevented virement between funds for equipment and salaries, the Council for National Academic Awards (CNAA) usually requires very specific information about resources when validating courses, and heads of departments and college committees normally want some account of what members of staff are doing.

Moving from Receiving Opinions to Discussing them
The UGC, CNAA, inspectors and college committees usually do more than seek information. They comment on it and they express their opinions. It is then a short step to seeking reactions to these comments and opinions. In other words it is a short step from being a responsive recipient to a responsive discussant; and as soon as the process of discussion has begun, so has the process of persuasion. The process of discussion has an educative effect upon its participants. The significant effect from the point of view of academic freedom is that during such discussion external agents will develop their opinions about what *ought* to happen. There is a thin line between discussion of the past and consultation about the future.

Moving from Informed Consultation to Receiving Guidance
The development of an opinion about what academics ought to do becomes a fifth phase in which discussion leads in turn to consultation, to suggestions,

to advice and to guidance (see Figure 4.1). The transitions from one to the other may be gradual and almost imperceptible, but the significance of each transition is a matter of opinion and the reader must decide for himself. While inspectors in schools were once inclined only to 'suggest' or even only to 'observe', more recently they have become 'advisors'. The UGC used to receive reports and respond to requests (it still does), but now it also sends letters of 'guidance'. By the nature of its job, it looks at the future, not only the past. Inevitably this makes it prescriptive unless it bends over backwards not to be.

FIGURE 4.1
The slippery slope of accountability

THE INSTITUTION	THE EXTERNAL AGENT
1 Gives a voluntary account	Receives an account
2 Is obliged to report formally	Requires an account
3 Is answerable	Asks questions
4 Receives external opinions	Expresses opinions to the institution
Responds to external opinions	Discusses opinions with the institution
5 Consults informally	Is consulted informally

Receives — suggestions
              advice
              guidance
	Suggests
	Advises
	Offers guidance

6 Voluntarily does as instructed	Gives instructions
7 Complies under threat	Controls

At what stage is academic freedom crucially infringed? It is perfectly possible for institutions and individuals to ignore the points, suggestions, advice and guidance put to them, but as we move from suggestions to guidance there is an increasing implication that compliance is expected, and with it, a diminution of freedom. Furthermore the freedom in question is increasingly, though not necessarily, academic freedom. The suggestions, advice and guidance are increasingly about academic matters, such as what is to be taught.

Personally I do not think that the activities of external agents in the phases so far described could be impugned on the grounds that they interfere with academic freedom. Indeed they may be supported by the principles of academic freedom itself. For the UGC, the CNAA or the DES have as much right to express their opinions and, indeed, to discuss them as part of their general civil liberties as other institutions, because in certain matters they too are commissioned to seek the truth. I am happy for external agents to express their opinions and to offer as much guidance as they like. My freedom is only reduced when my power to do what I want is reduced. Freedom is concerned with the ratio between an individual's desires and his powers to satisfy them.

Voluntary Agreement
It is when, and if, external organizations seek to impose their opinions upon the academic activities of others, that issues of academic freedom arise. It is when 'advice' becomes 'commands to be obeyed' that academics do not decide what to do for themselves and no longer exercise responsibility. On the slippery slope from having freedom to being controlled, the shift from 'guidance' to 'commands' seems to be critical because it is at this point that responsibility is transferred. Responsibility is resigned without a resignation from office.

For example, a university can, perhaps at some risk, decide not to follow the guidance offered by the UGC; but two cases were reported to the SRHE Leverhulme seminar in which a polytechnic and a university department could not refuse the dictates of a local education authority and a professional organization respectively about what they should teach. In these two cases academic freedom to decide the content of courses had been lost. I am not saying that it either should or should not have been lost, nor does it follow that freedom to take other associated decisions was lost. I am saying that there is no sharp line between freedom and unacceptable accountability; that nonetheless the examples demand an answer to the question 'In what circumstances should freedom and responsibility to take academic decisions be defended?'; that in order to answer this question it is necessary both to make a moral distinction and to distinguish pertinently between different circumstances; that both these distinctions are difficult to make; and to ease these difficulties, the criteria for distinguishing legitimate and illegitimate infringements of academic freedom will need to be defined more sharply in the 1980s than they have been in the past.

Compliance under Threat
There seems to me to be a distinction between an individual or an institution willingly resigning responsibility by letting an external agent take decisions (as in Level 6 in Figure 4.1), and complying with the wishes of an external agent under duress. An example of such duress might be the threat of a funding agency to withhold resources.

The differences lie not in what is done, but in the justification for doing it and the will of those who do it. If an institution is asked by its funding agency to close a specific department, the institution may decide on what it sees as the merits of the case (as in Level 5), it may comply because it recognizes and accepts the authority (not power) of the funding agency (as in Level 6), or it may acquiesce, recognizing the threat, sanction or power of the funding agency. In Level 6 the institution surrenders its responsibility because the reason for its action is not its judgements of the merits of the case. It could be possible for an institution to act responsibly, that is as a result of its own judgements and intentions, even though, coincidentally, complying with commands under duress. But when individuals or institutions no longer decide what they are going to do, and when some other organization, agent or individual has power to ensure that the individual or institution will do what it wishes, I believe that agent can be said to be in control. Not that control is ever entirely complete or absent. It is not an all-or-nothing factor. What is important is the level of detail at which influence is exerted. Funding for higher education has never been unlimited; hence there have always been some constraints upon freedom for academic developments, and there always will be. Conversely, not in the most autocratic regime would it be possible to control the detailed style and content of every tutorial. But to the extent that academic decisions are taken by people other than the teachers who have to implement them, academic freedom is lost.

What will require much greater clarification during the 1980s is the level of accountability teachers in higher education have and to whom. It is clear that they have some accountability to their employers and to their source(s) of funding (which may not be the same). In some subjects there is a measure of accountability to professional bodies representing their students' future employers. There is also some accountability to students and this, one may anticipate, will increase as staff/student relationships become less paternalistic and if courses become more negotiated.

If teachers in higher education are to be accountable at some level to employers, funding agencies, professional bodies and students, the level of accountability to any one of them cannot exceed Level 6 and would not normally exceed Level 5. For example a polytechnic lecturer cannot give a full explanation of a curriculum to his students (Level 1), or be answerable to a professional body (Level 3), if his local education authority controls (Level 7) the curriculum without consultation with him.

CONCLUSION

Entangled in these three issues of freedom, rights and accountability are two values that have run through virtually all the SRHE Leverhulme seminars: the need for flexibility and diversity, and the need to maintain and raise standards. The tension between these two values creates a corresponding tension between the accountability and freedom of teachers.

REFERENCES

Black, P.J. and Sparkes, J.J. (1982) Teaching and learning. Chapter 5 in Bligh, D.A. (Editor) *Professionalism and Flexibility for Learning* Guildford: Society for Research into Higher Education

Blume, S.S. (1982) A framework for analysis. In Oldham, G. (Editor) *The Future of Research* Guildford: Society for Research into Higher Education

Leavis, F.R. (1972) *Nor Shall my Sword* Chatto and Windus

National Union of Students and the National Council for Civil Liberties (1970) *Academic Freedom and the Law* London

Pincoffs, E.L. (1972) *The Concept of Academic Freedom* Austin: University of Texas Press

Searle, J. (1972) *The Campus War* Penguin Books

ACKNOWLEDGEMENTS

I am grateful to Professor John Dancy, Professor Gareth Williams, Dr Glenn Langford and Mr Tony Jaffey for helpful comments on drafts of this chapter.